Featherstone

FOUNDATIONS OF
MATHEMATICS

An active approach to number,
shape and measures in the Early Years

Carole Skinner and Judith Stevens

Published 2012 by Featherstone Education
Bloomsbury Publishing plc
50 Bedford Square, London, WC1B 3DP
www.bloomsbury.com

ISBN 978-1-8553-9-4360

Text © Carole Skinner and Judith Stevens 2012
Design © Lynda Murray
Photographs © Shutterstock, London Early Years Foundation/Emli Bendixen,
and Acorn Childcare Ltd.

British Library Cataloguing-in-Publication Data

Printed in China by C & C Offset Printing Co., Ltd.

10 9 8 7 6 5 4 3 2 1

This book is produced using paper that is made from wood grown in
managed, sustainable forests. It is natural, renewable and recyclable.
The logging and manufacturing processes conform to the environmental
regulations of the country of origin.

To see our full range of titles visit **www.bloomsbury.com**

Acknowledgements

Photographs with kind permission of London Early Years Foundation
and Acorn Childcare Ltd.

Contents

About the Authors

Carole Skinner is an early years maths specialist, a consultant and writer who believes that teaching, learning and encountering maths should be equally exciting for children and adults. She has taught in a range of inner city primary schools and nursery settings and spent time as a local authority advisor, national strategy consultant and university lecturer. She is a foundation associate of Early Education, one of the UK's leading educational charities for parents, carers and early years practitioners. Carole is particularly interested in encouraging children to be number-confident problem solvers and in using children's own interests as a springboard for understanding maths. In the last few years Carole has written several books and magazine articles on the themes of problem solving and learning maths outdoors. Recently she has been involved in the production of early years maths materials including a range of board and computer games for children.

Judith Stevens is an early learning consultant and author specialising in mathematics, communication and language. She has a diverse career in early years education, including involvement in the non-maintained sector as well as working as a teacher, maths coordinator and early years team leader. Following a long career in local authority advisory roles, Judith took on leadership roles in national programmes including 'Every Child a Talker'. Judith is a prolific writer and has written books about early years mathematics and early language, and numerous articles for early years magazines. As an independent consultant Judith has provided extensive support and training across England, Wales and Ireland. She is passionate about all aspects of maths, particularly maths outdoors and through stories, rhymes and role play. She believes that all children have the right to become confident, effective mathematicians and that talking about maths in the early years is a great way to begin this journey.

Acknowledgements

We would like to thank the children, parents and practitioners at Baring Primary School, Lewisham, for the wonderful images and for sharing their growing mathematical thinking and understanding with us.

Also the staff and children at Ridgeway Primary and Nursery School, Croydon, who enthusiastically trialled many of our ideas, games and activities and who gave us their artwork, especially Charlie, Jack, Theo and Ela.

We would also like to acknowledge the support, advice and friendship we have had from the many early years practitioners who have given so willingly their time and experience.

Introduction

As adults, we use mathematics all the time – whether we are checking how long it took to walk to the bus stop, scouring timetables for the next train, weighing ingredients for a cake, working out the number of rolls of wallpaper we still need, sorting out the washing, or fitting as much as possible into a suitcase! But not many of us would describe ourselves as mathematicians, and even fewer of us would proclaim ourselves to be confident mathematicians or 'good' at maths. However, although we may not see ourselves as mathematicians, we are constantly interacting with the numbers, shapes and measures in our everyday lives.

This book aims to demystify maths for non-maths specialists but also offer maths subject leaders and managers opportunities to reflect on how maths in their own school or setting is meeting the needs of young learners.

The content and the organization of the early years mathematical curriculum varies enormously worldwide. The statutory framework for the foundation years in England (EYFS 2012) has divided the whole of

mathematical development into two sections, quite simply: 'numbers', which includes all aspects of numbers as labels, for counting and calculating, and; 'shape, space and measures'. Problem solving is seen as encompassing both sections.

Parts of this book focus on the content of maths learning – what children learn. But it is equally important to reflect on how children learn – through playing and exploring, active involvement, and creating and thinking critically. Effective maths learning involves children in doing, thinking and playing, indoors and outdoors, with adults as co-players and children as co-planners of learning. In essence, learning maths is all about helping children to make sense of their mathematical world.

The first four chapters in the book each explore one key aspect of maths: numbers, calculating, shape and measures. Each chapter discusses the content of the maths, including the way in which children's understanding develops. There are hundreds of ideas for open-ended, practical, hands-on, fun experiences. Of course, it is down to you, as a professional, to decide which experiences will inspire the children you know best – building on what they already know and can do, and informed by their current interests and enthusiasms.

Each chapter concludes with reflections on the role of the adult, giving you opportunities to consider the best ways in which you can support young children's maths learning. Of course, you will plan to introduce experiences which focus specifically on aspects of maths learning. But you will also enhance the continuous learning provision, providing provocations for learning to ensure children have ongoing opportunities to explore their own mathematical fascinations. Each chapter also includes helpful hints for enhancing the learning environment and provision, and useful vocabulary lists. We all know the importance of talk in children's learning. After all, if they cannot talk about what they are doing and why, it will be very difficult for children to move on in their mathematical thinking. It will be even less likely that they will choose mathematical themes for their play or engage meaningfully in mathematical graphics.

The role of the adult also includes working together and engaging families, so there are some 'start up' ideas for 'Maths Home Challenges' at the end of each chapter. You could photocopy these and laminate them for children to take home and share with their families. Use your creativity to tailor the tasks and add photos or images to appeal to the children and families in your setting. The aim is to identify manageable ideas for children and parents to carry out together – whether it is matching pairs of socks, playing a game with coins or sinking boats in the bath. The emphasis is always on the process rather than the product, having fun and learning together. Occasionally, you may ask children to bring something back after the weekend to share or talk about what they have done and reinforce the maths learning.

The content of these chapters will offer many ideas for mathematical problem solving indoors and outdoors. We know that if children have opportunities to be involved in open-ended problem-solving experiences with familiar adults, they will begin to identify their own maths problems in their play and everyday life. One of the best things we can do is offer children an exciting, challenging learning environment where real problems arise naturally as part of everyday activities. That's why we have included a specific chapter (Chapter 5) which gives you the opportunity to really think about how you are supporting children to identify and solve problems which engage and inspire them.

Many children are also motivated by collections. Think about your own childhood. What did you collect? Shells, pebbles, stones, leaves, badges, postcards, dolls, cars, stickers or ladybirds and worms? Everyday collections can be wonderful starting points for sorting, exploring and investigating. That's why we have included a chapter that focuses on collecting and sorting. After all, we are much more likely to get truly involved in counting and calculating with things that really interest us – who would choose to play with identical plastic 'sorting' items when the contents of a shiny, exciting treasure chest or a collection of fascinating patterned wooden blocks, fabric and metal frogs beckon?

The most effective early years practitioners are proficient at identifying 'ways into learning' for children. They observe children's play and find out what inspires and motivates them. For many children (and adults) stories, books and rhymes are a good way into maths learning – often because they seem comfortable, and are of course fun when shared with a trusted, familiar adult. Chapter 7 focuses on the part stories and rhymes can play in children's mathematical development.

Maths outdoors should not be a replica of maths indoors – there is little point of plastic counting bricks or small threading activities on tables outdoors. So we have dedicated a whole chapter to focusing on developing this vital area of maths learning. Children learn about and understand more maths when their play includes den building, digging, using water hoses, climbing, making potions and gloop, and collecting bugs. They can play assorted games with opportunities to yell, sing, explore, experiment, marvel, discover, take risks and create without the limits imposed by being indoors. So when we are considering developing maths outdoors, we need to reflect on indoor experiences and think of ways to extend them outdoors, complementing and enhancing indoor provision and celebrating the unique qualities of the outdoor natural and built environment.

As we said at the beginning, we are constantly interacting with the numbers, shapes and measures in our everyday lives, but we may not see ourselves as mathematicians. Our aim as early years practitioners must be to nurture all children as confident, capable mathematicians for the future. We believe that the ideas, experiences and opportunities for reflection in Foundations of Mathematics can help you on your journey to making this happen.

Carole Skinner and Judith Stevens, Autumn 2012

Chapter 1

All about number

Keeping it personal — children using an outdoor number line which includes photos of their friends.

As adults, we use numbers all of the time – whether we are checking the time on clocks or watches, flagging down a bus, scouring train timetables, looking hopefully at lottery tickets or bemoaning our credit card or bank statements. We may not see ourselves as mathematicians, but we are constantly interacting with the numbers in our environment. Numbers are an essential part of everyday life, and we need to help children to become confident in their use and to make numbers work for them.

This chapter focuses on the importance of children knowing and saying number names, knowing number names in order and recognising numerals. It is vital that adults help children to understand that there is a correct order in which to say number names when counting. It is almost impossible to count anything accurately unless you know the number names in order, and knowing the right order is as important as knowing the number names themselves.

Children's understanding of number starts from birth and develops gradually. Babies as young as five months are aware of quantities, and notice changes in amounts of objects. Before the age of one year, children develop an awareness of number names, and with the right support

from the adults around them, use these in their speech as soon as they talk. Children hear talk all around them; they are introduced to number through opportunities that occur in everyday life.

When children learning English as an additional language (EAL) are developing understanding of counting in English they will also be developing an increasing knowledge of numbers in their own language. It is therefore important to make links with their learning at home as well as introducing number names in English.

We need to remember that some children aren't at all interested in small numbers such as one to ten – they want to explore big numbers such as hundreds, thousands and millions. These children may be more fascinated by telephone numbers or car registration plates than number rhymes.

It is essential to lay solid foundations in early mathematics. We want confident mathematicians who can use numbers in their everyday environment for labelling, quantifying and calculating. Counting is the significant aspect of children's understanding of number on which quantifying and calculating skills are built.

Research by Gelman and Gallistel (1978) first generated counting principles, which continue to inform practitioners and are referred to in the (then) DCSF publication, *Children Thinking Mathematically – essential knowledge for Early Years practitioners* (2009). As children's counting skills develop, they will begin to understand counting principles:

- **One-to-one correspondence – when children touch or point to each object individually as they count and match a number to each object that is being counted.**

- **The need for stable order – children will gradually find out that numbers need to be said in the same order.**

- **Abstraction – children may begin by counting objects like cars 'in the here and now', in front of them, but they will also realise that many things can be counted, such as claps or jumps.**

- **Order irrelevance – when counting a group of objects in a random layout, it doesn't matter where you start; whether you start at the top, bottom, middle or edges, the result is the same as long as each item is counted once.**

- **Cardinality – understanding that the last number counted indicates how many things are in the set.**

What to look for when observing young children's mathematical development – children's use of number words and numerals:

- **shows an interest in numbers in the environment**

- **refers to numbers that are meaningful to them**

- **uses number words during play**

- **demonstrates knowledge of the order of numbers**

- **records, using marks that they can interpret and explain**

- **shows interest in representing numbers**

Talk about number is vital to support children's understanding and learning. Children need lots of opportunities to hear, say and see number words – sometimes this will be just orally and aurally, and this is a very important focus. On other occasions, experiences will be linked to number recognition, counting objects and calculating. Number rhymes and number books play an essential role in supporting children's progression in saying number names in order, so adults need to plan a systematic approach to using number rhymes (see page 108).

As well as using cardinal numbers (used to show quantity) – 'one, two, three, four. . . ', children need opportunities to use ordinal numbers (which show order or rank) – 'first, second, third, fourth. . .'. One obvious use for ordinal numbers is in lists of instructions: 'First we crack the egg, second we whisk it, third we sift in the flour. . .'. Ordinal numbers can also be used effectively during outdoor play, for example when racing and engaging in obstacle courses. Some children find ordinal numbers confusing, particularly the special cases such as 'first', 'second' and 'third'. 'Fourth', 'sixth' and 'seventh' can seem easier to use, but some children simply confuse cardinal and ordinal numbers e.g. 'five' and 'fifth'.

Numbers in order

Many three-year-olds entering a group care setting will know some number names. Some will know lots of number names and will even be able to recite some number names in order. This may come out as 'onetwothreefour. . .' as if it is one word, and the child may not actually realise that this is several words strung together, or that the individual words have meaning.

We know that, particularly before the age of seven, children's vocabulary growth is largely determined by parental practice (Biemiller, 2003) and this applies to number words too. Children learn number names by hearing familiar adults using number names in familiar and meaningful contexts.

We often observe children using number words when they are engaged in imaginative and pretend play, e.g. in the role-play café – 'three buns, seventeen-twenty biscuits and two coffees'. They have conversations with other children involving number words, sometimes including letter names, without differentiating. Telephones can stimulate the use of number words, with children using strings of unrelated numbers when they answer the phone 'sevententhreetwo', although this is becoming less frequent as fewer adults model this use of telephone numbers when picking up a phone.

Children need lots of opportunities to explore number names spontaneously and as part of their play before they begin to put numbers in the correct order. Practitioners need to support children's use of number words and show that they value this and take it seriously. So when children say, 'I've got six cars' the response could be, 'you've got six cars and I've got three cars', with the emphasis on the label, rather than comparison or actual counting of objects. Adults need to observe and extend play when children use number strings in role play. For example, child: 'is this 468, 3957?'; adult: 'yes this is 468, 3957. Do you want to order a pizza – we have a three for two offer.'

Practitioners should take all opportunities to use number words in everyday conversation too, with a focus on the word, rather than always counting things: 'oh, there is only one chair left at the table'; 'look, there are three snails eating the lettuce'; 'it's nearly three o'clock now'; 'we've got seventeen children with packed lunches'.

At first, children may tune into the rhythmic sound of counting – 'one, two, three, four, five', but attempt to count using familiar number names – perhaps the ages of their brothers, sisters or friends, for example, with a number sequence of 'five, six, three, six, three. . .'. The focus at this stage is not on whether the number names are in the correct order, but rather the 'feel' of the words, an important part of 'word play'. Usually, children can say a number sequence e.g. 'one, two, three, four, five', before they can count the same number of objects accurately.

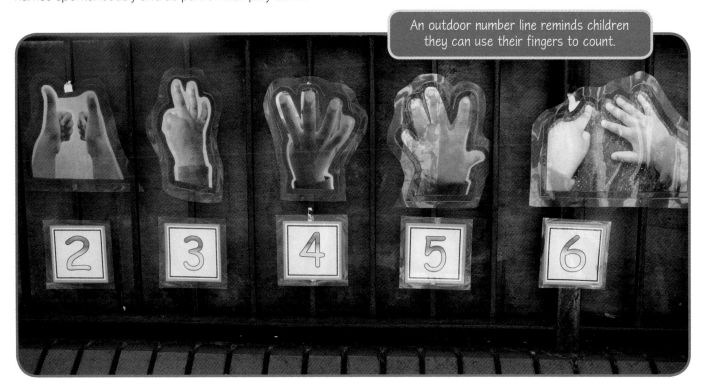

An outdoor number line reminds children they can use their fingers to count.

There are several potential difficulties in children learning number names in order:

- **not separating number names – creating a string**

- **missing out number names**

- **repeating number names**

- **using correct names, but in the wrong order**

- **using number names in the correct order when starting from one or zero, but not when starting from another number**

- **confusing 'teen' words and 'ty' words e.g. fifteen and fifty**

- **extending three and five to 'threeteen' and 'fiveteen' rather than 'thirteen' and 'fifteen'**

In essence, children learn number names in order by saying number names in order, through counting along with an adult, joining in with number rhymes and songs. As they gain confidence, they move from saying number sequences to five, and then ten and then backwards from ten to zero. Finally they move towards saying the number that comes after any number to ten, and then beyond. Saying, chanting, singing, whispering, calling, shouting and echoing number counts helps children to learn number names in the right order.

An exciting, imaginative play scenario offers lots of opportunities for counting interesting objects.

How many toadstools can you find?

Numbers in order — experiences and activities

I know that number

Talk about number names with children – what numbers do they know? Why is the number important to them? For many children important numbers will be their door number, telephone numbers, car registration plates, a familiar bus number, their age or the age of a favourite friend or sibling (often the age they want to be). Support children as they talk about their number and encourage other children to talk about the same number too. Other children will be fascinated by huge numbers and will want to talk about millions of stars.

Number snap

This is a noisy activity to play outdoors. Decide on the numbers which can be used e.g. only numbers 'one to five' or numbers 'two to ten'. Tell the children that they will hear some music. When the music stops, they have to call out one number name, and then move around repeating it until they find another person saying the same number name. When they find a partner, they both sit down. This continues until all the children still standing are saying different numbers, and those children are 'out'. Continue until there is just one pair of children left, or no pairs of matching numbers.

Parachute numbers

This is a large group or whole class activity and children need to be familiar with parachute games. All the children hold the parachute edge. Number the children one to ten. As the children move the parachute up and down, call out one number. All the children with that number run under the parachute and change places. Try calling two numbers at once, but make sure there are enough children holding the parachute. Let a child take the lead at calling number names.

One, two, three, four, five rhyme

Introduce the traditional rhyme:

One, two, three, four, five,

once I caught a fish alive.

Six, seven, eight, nine, ten,

then I let it go again.

Chant the rhyme together – this isn't about counting objects or calculating, but simply focusing on the rhythm of the numbers in the correct order.

Puppet mistakes – number names

Many early years practitioners use puppets to support early language development. Puppets can be really helpful in supporting children with maths, so consider acquiring a special maths character puppet which alerts children to group maths activities. In this case, the puppet is going to use some correct number words but also words which are not number names. Choose a sign for children to indicate a mistake, e.g. an animal noise such as a 'squeak' or give each child a shaker. The puppet starts correctly: 'seven', 'three', 'six', 'apple', or 'eight', 'one', 'six', 'tortoise' and children must indicate when they hear a word that is not a number name. Let the children take the lead.

Puppet mistakes – number names in order

Once the children are familiar with the special maths puppet using number names, there are lots of ways to extend the activity. In this case, the puppet is going to use correct number names, but not necessarily in the correct order. Rather than asking children to call out, give each child a small red laminated card. When the puppet says a number in the wrong order, children have to hold up the red card. When the group are very familiar with the activity, you can support small groups as they carry out the game independently. When the children are competent in counting in ones, encourage them to teach the puppet to count in twos, fives and tens.

Clapping and slapping

Start a clapping game with the children: clap hands together once, then slap your hands on your thighs once. Continue the rhythm until all the children are confident about joining in. Then begin to say number names in the correct order, saying one number name on each slap of your thighs. When you reach five (or ten), stop and start again. As the children become more confident, when you reach the designated number, say the number names in reverse order.

Missing numbers

Create a short daily routine at a group or circle time. Chant numbers to ten (or twenty) in the correct order, using an action with each number name e.g. moving both hands in the air from right to left. When many children are familiar chanting the numbers, set a challenge. Ask the children to listen carefully and chant the numbers, at some stage missing out one number e.g. 'one, two, three, four, six'. Keep the rhythm going, and encourage the children to identify the omission with a pre-arranged sign – for example, pressing their nose and saying 'beep beep' or tapping the top of their head and saying 'ooops'.

Number trains

This is a whole class activity for outdoors or hall time. Divide the class into three groups, and give each child in the group a number from one to ten. The idea is to form a number train. Each group has to move around the area (outside, coloured chalked 'tracks' can be added) and wait for a signal (a train whistle is ideal). At the first signal, numbers one (the engine) and two (a carriage) must link up. At the next whistle, number three joins on, and so on until more and more carriages are added.

Starting points

When children are confident in saying number names in order from one to ten (or twenty), you should plan lots of opportunities using different starting points. Model the experience starting at 'three' or 'seven' and as children gain in confidence, ask individual children to choose a starting point.

Counting

On many occasions, we don't need to know the exact number of things – it is enough to know that there are several eggs left, half a box of teabags or a few apples. We estimate or guess and that is all that is needed.

But there are times when we do need to know the exact number of items and to count accurately, and this is something that all adults do in everyday life – counting out ten pence pieces, stitches in knitting or items for a special offer, e.g. 'Buy six for £4.99'.

Of course, we also all know that sometimes we see a small number of items and we recognise how many there are without counting – in mathematical terms 'we are able to identify the number of randomly placed objects in a group rapidly, confidently and accurately, without counting'. This ability is known as 'subitising' and most adults can subitise about five or six objects. We know that children as young as two years of age can subitise two or three objects and many of three and four years old are subitising four objects.

You can try this out yourself – throw a small handful of objects in a random formation and see whether you 'know' how many there are, or whether you need to count them. Of course, this sometimes means that when children are counting a larger number of items in a group, they may not start counting at one; they may see four together and then begin to count onwards from five.

Counting reliably is much more than saying number names in the right order. To be able to count, children need to be able to:

- **say number names in order**

- **say one number name for each item and remember what they have counted**

- **know that the last number they say is the number of objects in the group**

What is more, they need to do all of these activities at the same time.

Children need to be motivated to count for a purpose and there are generally two main purposes for counting: when we need to find out an exact number, rather than an estimate e.g. 'we need six slices of apple for six children'; and when we need to check that there are exactly the same number of things e.g. 'there are six children, but only five cushions'.

Recent research (Gunderson and Levine, 2011) has identified the essential nature of parents' number talk. The researchers found that parents' number talk that involves counting or labelling sets of present, visible objects impacts on children's later cardinal-number knowledge e.g. knowing that the word 'five' refers to sets of five entities. Other types of parent number talk were not seen to be related to children's later knowledge in the same way.

In addition, number talk that refers to large sets of present objects (i.e. sets of size four to ten that fall outside children's ability to track individual objects) is more predictive of children's later cardinal-number knowledge than talk about smaller sets. That is to say, for example, a parent exploring a large number of assorted toy cars or animals with a child and talking about seven, eight or nine of those, rather than focusing on between one and five objects, which is often the case. This really has implications for the advice we give to families about the sorts of activities they can carry out at home with children to support knowledge and understanding of cardinal numbers.

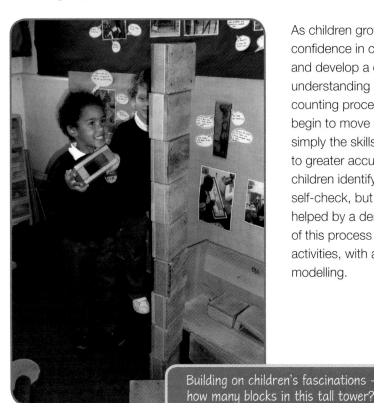

Building on children's fascinations – how many blocks in this tall tower?

As children grow in confidence in counting and develop a clear understanding of the counting procedure, they will begin to move away from simply the skills of counting to greater accuracy. Some children identify the need to self-check, but others will be helped by a demonstration of this process in hands-on activities, with a practitioner modelling.

Counting – experiences and activities

Counting in pretend play

Children often count very naturally as part of their pretend play. Provide lots of objects to support counting and extend role-play and imaginative-play provision. Provide a new toy puppy. What does he need? Four bone-shaped biscuits, three walks a day, two tins of food, one dog basket.

Toppling towers challenge

Many young children love to build high towers using wooden blocks and these are often used to compare heights. Set a 'terrific towers' challenge and support children as they count the number of blocks they have piled one on top of the other. Who can build a tower using the most blocks before it topples over?

Handfuls

Counting can be linked to estimation and this activity can be differentiated to meet the needs of all children. Before the day, get children to make both a right and left painted handprint on A4 card. It is worth laminating the cards, as they can be used over and over again. Provide a basket of natural objects of a similar size e.g. conkers. Ask one child how many they predict they can pick up with one hand, then after they have done so, let them try and place the conkers on the handprint. Support the child as they count how many conkers they have picked up, then ask them to predict again for the other hand. Is it the same number of conkers? Some children will find it helpful to match the conkers to the fingers on the handprints and this will encourage them to use their fingers to support counting.

Treasure chests

Provide small treasure boxes (old jewellery boxes are good). Put play gold nuggets and 'jewels' in dry sand and encourage children to sieve for treasure and fill the treasure boxes. How many jewels can they find? Alternatively, place the jewels in a shallow tray of dry sand (try adding glitter for interest) for children to move with plastic tweezers.

Magic beans

Prepare the 'magic beans': spread 500 grams of dried butter beans on several layers of newspaper, outdoors or in a well-ventilated room. Spray one side of the beans with non-toxic spray paint – perhaps gold. The beans can be used in place of dice in many games, e.g. throw six beans, count the number that land gold side upwards and move that number of spaces.

What's in the box?

Prepare five small boxes. Place a number of small objects in each box – between one and five or between one and ten (you could use magic beans). Ask children to choose a box, shake it and predict how many are inside. Open the box and count to confirm. Extend the activity by putting the same number of items in two of the boxes and asking children to predict which two boxes have the same number of objects.

Dinosaur dig

Hide model dinosaurs in a damp sand tray. Introduce as part of explorer pretend play and encourage children to predict how many dinosaurs they will find. Take turns to dig for the dinosaurs – count them together.

Baking by numbers

We all know that cooking and in particular baking, are great experiences to support early measures. But if you use 'cups' and 'spoons' as measures instead of weighing using grams, children will then need to count carefully. Emphasize the counting aspect of the experience, e.g. while making cakes.

Ingredients:

- 3 eggs

- 3 cups self-raising flour

- 3 tablespoons margarine

- 1 cup milk

- 1 cup sugar

- 1 cup currants

Method:

Step 1: Cream butter and sugar together.

Step 2: Add flour alternately with milk and currants.

Step 3: Place spoonfuls on a tray.

Step 4: Bake at 200°C for 10 minutes.

Number rhymes

It's really important that children have daily opportunities to interact with 'core' number rhymes (see Chapter 7 page 108). Many number rhymes encourage children to use their fingers to represent items e.g. five current buns, five speckled frogs, five little ducks. When using rhymes with the children, ensure they recount from one e.g. counting the ducks one, two, three, four, five. Alternatively, give the children opportunities to move their whole bodies physically as part of the rhymes – being 'jumping frogs' or 'tiptoeing elephants'.

Puppet mistakes – counting

The children need to be familiar with the special maths puppet and know that sometimes, they need to correct the puppet's counting mistakes. We all know that if children are emotionally engaged in an activity, it supports their learning. In this case, they want the puppet to get the right answer and they want to help.

Children know the puppet isn't 'real' but they engage in the pretend play. Make sure all the children can see the items that the puppet is 'counting' and set the scene accordingly. Create an agreed signal for the children when the puppet makes a mistake – try to avoid hand waving or calling out. The puppet can make different sorts of mistakes – double counting an item, missing an item, missing a number, not starting at 'one'. Try to give the children lots of practice at identifying one sort of error and ask them to give the puppet 'hints' to remember what to do.

Mrs Wolf

This is a variation on a traditional favourite and is best played outdoors or in a large hall. It also supports early talk about 'time' as part of measures. Share the rules for the game – the children have a 'home' area at one side of the space; the wolf has a 'home' area some way away. The aim is for the children to sneak up on the wolf without being caught.

Start with an adult leading as 'Mrs Wolf', standing with their back facing the group of children. The children chant 'What's the time, Mrs Wolf?' and the wolf calls back any 'o'clock' from one to twelve e.g. when the answer is 'seven o'clock', the children take seven steps towards Mrs Wolf, counting out loud. When the answer is 'dinner time', the children run for home and the wolf chases them. Any child successfully reaching the wolf before 'dinner time' is called, becomes the wolf. As soon as the children are familiar with the game, a child can take the lead from the beginning.

Recognising numerals

Children need lots of opportunities to count, say, recognise and identify numbers. There are numerals all around us, and some children will notice them spontaneously, showing an awareness of and interest in numbers in their environment e.g. house numbers, bus numbers and clocks. These children may demonstrate their curiosity by offering comments such as, 'that's ten, the same as my door' or asking questions – 'what's this number?'; 'why is four on the door?'. For some children, numbers are exciting and fascinating and they talk about them a lot. But although we are surrounded by numbers, this can sometimes pass some children by, and merge into the general melee of colours, shapes, signs, symbols, pictures and images in the environment. Adults need to be very aware of those children who need support in identifying numbers.

Numerals are symbols which represent numbers, so 'five' and 'seventy-five' are written in numerals as '5' and '75'.

Some three-year-olds entering a group care setting will already recognise individual numerals of personal significance. But for many, the first numeral they recognise is around their fourth birthday – they will recognise the '4' on their birthday cards in a way in which they did not notice numerals when they received cards on their third birthday.

Recognising numerals is not as easy as it may seem – there are so many different styles and fonts that some numerals can be very confusing for some children e.g. 1, 7 and 4. Children who are unfamiliar with handwriting may fail to recognise handwritten versions of computer-generated numerals. It is really important that adults model numeral formation on a daily basis. As children get older, they may be very confident with the recognition of numerals to '9', but have difficulty when numbers are represented by two digits e.g. reading 17 as 'one, seven' rather than 'seventeen'.

Number lines are key to supporting children's recognition of numerals. Most early years environments include number lines and number tracks, but they are often not used effectively. Many are located high on the wall, rather than at child height; others have numbers missing or obscured by furniture or are simply 'part of the wallpaper' and ignored by adults and children.

The most effective number lines are the ones made with children. Make A4 number cards by printing one numeral on each card, with a large square underneath, and laminate the cards separately. Then stick the correct number of photographs of children on each card e.g. six faces on numeral '6'. Fix these cards in the correct order, at child height, with a 'washing line' underneath and supply an identical set of cards for children to match in the correct order. These meaningful visual clues will support children's thinking and inspire them. After all, there are few things children are more interested in than themselves and their friends. Ensure that you refer to the number line on a daily basis, and support children as they use it independently. As children begin to show less interest, change the 'clues' to other interesting items. As children gain in confidence, you can remove the fixed number line and support children as they peg the numerals in the correct order on the washing line. Older children will not always need the visual clues and will begin to recognise the numerals and place them in the correct order independently.

Number tracks are useful because children can put objects on them. Number tracks drawn outdoors are even more helpful as children can actually move themselves along the track – by walking, hopping or jumping. If adults can model games, such as 'I am on number four and I am going to hop to number six', children are more likely to incorporate number tracks into their play.

Charlie said computers need passwords. So he drew a computer and invented a password for the 'vet's office'.

Recognising numerals — experiences and activities

Pretend play — farms and zoos

Enhance pretend play by providing numerals on signs with fields and farm animals or cages and wild animals e.g. 4 cows, 5 horses, 6 sheep. As an extension, add signs with images of animals, small numerals on separate cards and blu-tack for children to create their own signs. Alternatively, support children as they write their own numerals.

Car play

Make laminated numeral labels for each large wheeled toy outdoors. Draw 'parking bays' with the children and label one for each wheeled toy. Support children as they 'park' each vehicle at tidy up time. Indoors, provide labelled parking bays for toy cars, label the cars and provide children with a petrol station, ramps and a road mat. Provide additional numerals to support pretend play – a car wash, car park or petrol pumps with prices, road signs and bus stops with numerals. Encourage children to make their own signs to support pretend play.

Number walk — indoors

Plan a number walk around the early years setting to ensure there are numerals to see. Provide digital cameras for a small group of children to use to record the numerals. As you spot numerals, take turns to take photos. Identify the numerals together. Possible numerals include: clocks, room numbers, calendars, tray numbers. Print the photos out with the group and help children as they report back to another group of children. Set a challenge for individual children to find the location of the numerals.

Numeral lotto

Use the images from the number walks to create a lotto game. You will need at least 24 different images.

1. Print two copies of four A4 sheets, each with six separate images.

2. Laminate one copy of each A4 sheet to create the base boards and then cut the duplicates into 24 individual cards and laminate these separately.

3. Place all the individual cards face down and take turns to select a card. What is the numeral (s)? Who has the identical numeral on their base board?

Number hunt — outdoors

Extend the indoor number walk for a small group by exploring the local environment. Include meaningful numerals for children – house and shop numbers, bus numbers, road numbers e.g. A21, prices in shop windows, bus times. Take lots of photos of the numerals. Now create a number hunt for the other children. Provide an A4 sheet of the photos and a clipboard for each pair of children. The challenge is to find the numeral in the image, and record where it is found – in words, or through digital images showing the location.

Obstacle course

Set up an obstacle course in the outdoor area. Label a route with numerals – which obstacle is 1st (first), 2nd (second) or 3rd (third)? When children are proficient in following the course in the correct order, try going in the opposite direction, starting at the end and going back to the first obstacle.

Number line game

You need:

- ten laminated A4 cards with numerals 1–10. Each card should have a square on it.

Place the cards face down on the table. Provide ten baskets, each containing ten small linked items e.g. plastic spiders, centipedes, ladybirds. Each child selects a card in turn. They identify the numeral, then choose a basket of items and count these out to match the numeral, e.g. counting seven spiders for the numeral '7'. Firmly fix the spiders to the square on the card using blu-tack. Carry on in the same way until all the items are fixed on to the cards. With the children, peg the cards on a washing line in the correct order. Refer to the number line on a daily basis.

Pop-up heads

1. Fold a piece of A4 card in half lengthways.

2. Now draw lines dividing the card into ten equal parts across the width.

3. Write the numerals 1–10 in the bottom half of each space.

4. Provide one copy of the card for each child and help them to cut vertical lines to the middle, creating ten 'flaps' above the numerals. Each child draws ten faces, one on each flap. Children can use these Pop-up heads to support their independent counting and numeral recognition.

Chalking games

You need:

- playground chalk
- ten A4 cards with numerals 1-10

Chalk ten circles on the ground outdoors. Write one numeral from 1–10 in each circle. With a large group, try out moving in different ways to music, e.g giant strides, pigeon steps, rabbit hops, kangaroo jumps. Call out a mode of travelling for children to move around the outdoor area. When the music stops, hold up a numeral card and the children have to hop/jump/stride to the circle indicated. The last child(ren) to the circle sit out the next round. Continue until only one child remains. As an extension, support children as they write numerals in the circles.

Numbers in the air

Before they can write numerals, children need lots of opportunities to develop their gross motor skills and form numerals by writing in the air on a large scale. Provide a laundry basket full of scarves, lengths of sheer, light fabric and ribbons for children to select from. Ask the children to hold their choice in one hand and draw a circle in the air, then ask them to draw it in the other direction e.g. clockwise then anti-clockwise. Change hands and repeat. Now ask them to draw a line in the air up and down (vertically) and from side to side (horizontally), with one hand and then the other. When the children are confident drawing lines and circles, begin to form numerals. Let individual children take the lead for others to identify and copy.

Spells for cauldrons

Provide laminated 'spells', with plastic/fabric toys, natural objects, a cauldron and a wooden spoon e.g.

2 rats, 3 spiders, 4 fir cones, 5 conkers

Provide 'blank' writing formats with suggestions for ingredients and sticky label numerals for children to create their own 'spells'. Support children as they use marks to record independently.

Mathematical mark-making

In the *'Independent Review of Mathematics Teaching in Early Years Settings and Primary Schools'* (2008), Williams stated (Chapter 3, page 34):

'The EYFS guidance stresses the value of children's own graphic explorations, and it is common to see children from an early age making their own marks in role-play to communicate or act out activities they observe in adults, such as writing letters or making lists. It is comparatively rare, however, to find adults supporting children in making mathematical marks as part of developing their abilities to extend and organise their mathematical thinking. While 'emergent writing' is a recognised term, that is not the case for 'emergent mathematical mark-making'. This misses a valuable opportunity to encourage early experimentation.'

He advised that,

Early years practitioners should encourage mathematical mark-making and open ended discussion (or sustained shared thinking) in children's mathematical development'.

This informed the fourth of the ten recommendations of the Review and led to the development of two publications: *Mark Making Matters: Young children making meaning in all areas of learning and development (DCSF, 2008)* and *Children thinking mathematically: essential knowledge for Early Years practitioners (DCSF, 2009)*.

Practitioners need to be aware that in the same way that children are unlikely to write stories unless they tell stories and talk about stories, children are unlikely to make mathematical marks (sometimes referred to as mathematical graphics) unless they talk about numbers, space, shapes and measures in their play. Talking about maths underpins the development of mathematical thinking and mark-making supports this development.

Some ways in which practitioners can support mathematical mark-making

* Recognising the importance of children's mark-making in supporting the development of their mathematical thinking.

* Monitoring and reviewing provision for mathematics, including mark-making.

* Using and referring to numerals in the environment.

* Creating a culture which explicitly values mathematical mark-making.

* Making the most of routines to support mathematical thinking – lunch time, drinks, snacks, computer use, feeding class pets, cooking.

* Modelling use of open questions and discussions.

* Identifying and using specific mathematical vocabulary and getting involved in mathematical shared sustained thinking.

* Scaffolding, questioning, discussing, demonstrating and recording with children, and solving problems together.

* Identifying problems which suggest opportunities for recording, e.g. 'today is our stock-taking day – we need to count everything in our nursery. I don't know how we will remember everything.'

* Valuing children's mark-making and celebrating creativity.

* Supporting children as they share their mathematical thinking with peers.

* Demonstrating recording – using numerals and other marks: notes, tallying, drawings and symbols.

* Making no assumptions about children's marks and realizing they are as likely to be about numerals as about letters and words – supporting them as they explain.

* Using re-casting effectively – repeating back children's talk about their mathematical thinking, keeping their meaning and expanding and clarifying sensitively where appropriate.

* Displaying and sharing children's mathematical graphics.

* Sharing the importance of mathematical mark-making with families.

* Creating opportunities for mark-making throughout the indoor and outdoor environment, providing easy access to resources – particularly where children are identifying and solving mathematical problems.

* Providing access to clipboards, whiteboards and markers throughout the environment.

* Providing oppportunities to make temporary marks: water and brushes, marks in sand/soil, chalks, gelboards, charcoal or temporary creative collections.

The role of the adult

Most of children's understanding about numbers comes from talking about numbers and using numbers as part of everyday play indoors and outdoors. Practitioners need to consider very carefully: the environment they provide, including ways in which to enrich continuous provision; specific activities planned to support children's understanding of number; the vocabulary they introduce and model the use of; and the enabling statements and open-ended questions they ask.

These experiences and activities particularly help children understand about number:

- **exploring the language of number in practical situations**

- **using number names in pretend play and role play**

- **engaging in activities where numbers are important**

- **estimating the amount of items in interesting bags and boxes**

- **playing with numbers in rhymes and songs**

- **counting the contents of boxes or bags or even segments in oranges**

- **investigating written numerals in recipes, or on calendars, diaries, telephone directories or car number plates**

- **using number lines and number tracks**

- **making their own number lines and number tracks**

Making connections between fantasy play and home experiences, using graphics to support understanding.

Will spent a long time on the graphics table on his return to school. He told Mrs. Courtman that he was drawing his castle that was a present he was given for Christmas. He wanted to take his drawing home and agreed that a photocopy could go up on display.

"It's a castle! It's got lots of windows but mine has only got four."
Will 10.01.2011

Enriching provision

There is often a lot of discussion about communication-friendly spaces as practitioners reflect on the best way to develop areas of provision, indoors and outdoors, to support children's communication and language. In the same way, we need to develop the learning environment to support all aspects of children's mathematical development.

Areas of provision, indoors and outdoors, will vary within individual settings, but are highly likely to include the following areas or learning zones. Experiences in the outdoor area will reflect and enhance indoor provision, but will often be on a larger, noisier or messier scale, utilizing the natural or built environment (see Chapter 8, Maths Outdoors)

Practitioners may wish to consider the Aide memoire (page 133) at the end of the book before identifying areas for development.

Indoors	Outdoors
Mark-making	Mark-making
Sound making and music	Sound making and music
Small world play	Small equipment
Construction play	Large construction
Home corner	Play house and role play
Role play	Wheeled toys
Creative area	Large scale painting
Maths workshop	Climbing
Water play	Water play
Book area	Sand pit
Sand play	Digging area
	Growing area

Resource trays in all areas of provision should be clearly labelled with words and pictures (or real objects) so that all adults and children know where to find resources and, more importantly, where to return them. Practitioners may also choose to label some trays with numerals e.g. small world play resources: every tray labelled with a green label, the word and a numeral, so trays could be '1. farm animals'; '2. wooden people'; '3. emergency vehicles', with a relevant picture clue.

All areas of provision can be enhanced to support children's number development, but here are some ideas:

Home corner

Ensure children have access to resources which include written numerals to support their pretend and role-play:

- clocks, watches

- mobile phones, phones, telephone directories,

- address books, postcards, greetings cards

- calendars, diaries and appointment cards

- recipe books and cards

- shopping lists and receipts

Role-play

All role-play areas should include multiple copies of resources to support accurate counting e.g. a role-play shop should include multiple:

- real root vegetables including potatoes

- cereal boxes

- egg boxes

- shopping bags and purses

- empty washing up liquid, washing liquid and fabric softener containers

- plastic milk bottles

Open-ended questions and enabling statements about number

We all know the importance of talk in providing the foundations for mathematical learning. When we are supporting children's developing knowledge and understanding of number, we can introduce specific vocabulary and use questions which extend learning and enabling statements which will support children's thinking.

> I wonder if anyone can guess the number of bugs Mr Frog has eaten?

> I can see six apples on the tree.

> What can you tell me about your favourite number?

> How could we record the number of dinosaurs in the box?

> I'm wondering why Pedro Puppet has said there are five frogs?

> Why is that number so important?

> How many blocks can we build up before they all topple over?

Essential vocabulary about number

- ✦ **Count**
- ✦ **Number**
- ✦ **Numeral**
- ✦ **Zero**
- ✦ **One, two, three. . .**
- ✦ **Eleven, twelve, thirteen. . .**
- ✦ **Twenty, thirty, forty. . .**
- ✦ **Hundred, thousand, million**
- ✦ **First, second, third. . .**
- ✦ **Before, after, next**
- ✦ **Forwards, backwards**

Maths home challenges

Rockets

Find some empty cardboard boxes and packets and pile them up to build a rocket. How high can you build it together?

Now, count down together –

5, 4, 3, 2, 1, Blast off!

Take turns to knock the 'rocket' down.

Now build it up again.

Have fun!

Counting game

Find somewhere outdoors to play. Stand a distance away from each other and take turns to call out a number between one and three. If you say 'three', your child takes three steps towards you, counting together as they go.

Keep going until you reach each other for a hug!

Help your child to make up new rules for the game – you could both move at the same time, or you could change the way of moving – 'three jumps' or 'three hops'. Or you could choose bigger numbers – 'ten pigeon steps'.

Have fun!

Number fun

You will need:

* A pair of scissors

* Some catalogues, magazines and cards with numerals on

* A glue stick

* Some paper

Look through the magazines and cards together and talk about the numerals (written numbers) you see. Your child will be more interested in some than others, e.g. four-year-olds will like the numeral '4', or your child may recognise their door number, a bus number, or someone else's age.

Praise your child for every numeral they recognise and when they don't recognise one, say it together.

Cut out your favourite numerals and stick them on a piece of paper.

Bring the paper back here on Monday so that we can all share them.

Have fun together!

Included: glue stick, A4 paper, child's scissors

Doing calculations

Calculating experiences in the early years should include opportunities to add, subtract, compare, multiply and divide in hands-on situations. The first calculation strategies young children use are related to the play they are involved in or the practical happenings they observe in everyday life. When they play, children usually encounter and solve addition and subtraction problems by physically putting two groups together or actually taking an object away. They are unlikely to focus long on how many altogether and they rarely recount to find or check the resulting total. Comparison for young children is initially visual and it is only as counting knowledge develops that children use one-to-one correspondence to compare and find the difference between two numbers.

On the other hand early multiplication ideas develop quite quickly as children count groups of objects and sharing or doubling and halving is achieved mostly on a "one for you and one for me" distribution system.

In a mathematically challenging environment children will experience all these calculation ideas and begin to consider whether their calculations are sensible during practical activities such as putting together two collections of conkers, taking away some bricks from the

pile and dealing out cards during a game, doubling the number of beads they give each other.

At these early stages it is important to help children make links between the different aspects of calculation such as the relationship between addition and subtraction; this will support children who are starting to make those connections to begin understand the more difficult comparison and difference situations. Calculating experiences should include those that offer children the chance to find out 'how many are left' when some objects are removed or use a number line to practice the skill of counting up from one number to another to find out how many are missing. However, children's understanding of calculations will always be richer if they bump into those calculations when engaged in practical activities

Children will also tune into calculating while in conversation with their peers and with adults as they use the language associated with calculation. Playing maths games with dice and counters provides an ideal way to use words and phrases such as 'add', 'more than', double and 'altogether'. Our role as adults is to introduce and extend the children's calculation vocabulary by using it in stories and rhymes and other everyday situations.

Using number lines and tracks for calculations

Number tracks are a great visual and physical tool for young learners as they begin to understand calculation. On a number track each number or picture occupies a space. Number tracks start at one and can be vertical, horizontal or zigzag like a 100 square or a snakes and ladder board. You will notice that when children are using a zigzag track, many find counting or jumping along it in different directions confusing. This is usually because they are not yet secure in the order of numbers. They become even more uncertain as to which direction to move in when you include the hazard of climbing ladders or sliding down snakes.

On the whole when they are using a number track, children find addition in the form of 'counting on' easier to do than subtraction or finding the difference by 'counting back'. Using and understanding a number track will support the development of both counting on and counting back skills. However, many children with little experience of playing board games that use dice and a number track will often count the space they are on as a move rather than the jumps they make. You can help overcome this misconception by using a large number track on the floor and playing games where children throw a dice and then actually jump themselves along the track. You could also feature stepping stones across a pretend stream with children saying how many jumps they are going to make across the stones. This offers an alternative way of introducing the idea of a number track.

Number lines (unlike tracks) include a zero and have marks along the line to show the position of the numbers. Make sure that children are aware that although number lines usually start at zero and go from left to right, they can use just a section of a number line if they want to. They can also start their line from whichever numeral they wish. Young children need to have access to both number tracks and lines when they are playing and working with calculations; this will develop their mental imagery as well as being a good way into recording their calculations.

Children's own number lines support calculating.

Using dominoes for calculation

Large dominoes are always a very useful tool to demonstrate counting, addition and if the two halves of the domino are compared, children can tackle difference too. Sort out the dominoes together and talk about what's the same and what's different about them. Draw children's attention to the fact that some dominoes have spots in both halves and some have no spots in one half. You could suggest that the children sort out all the dominoes with spots that add to seven. Observe which children look at the domino and 'know' or mentally add the lower numbers such as three and one or two and two, and which children count all the spots on the domino each time; this will give you valuable insight into their growing knowledge of calculation. Providing two boxes labelled 'these domino spots add to 7 and these domino spots do not add to 7' will support children's sorting and calculation skills.

On another occasion children might decide to sort the dominoes in a different way. You could offer wooden numerals or number cards to those who want to record

how many dominoes they have in their collections. If children find it difficult to predict what will happen, discuss results with them and offer your own predictions, e.g. "I wonder how we could work out how many dominoes there will be if you collect all the double dominoes"; "Do you think there will be more than four?"

Adding

You will find that of the many calculation experiences children have during the early years, it is usually addition scenarios that they find the easiest to grasp and understand.

There are two types of addition situations that children usually encounter in the early years: first the more easily understood – combining – where two sets are put together to make a new set. Here, the statement 'I wonder how many there are altogether' is appropriate. Second is the addition scenario of counting up, where an original amount is increased resulting in a new total; in these situations you will often then hear comments such as 'Look how many I have now'.

In counting up it is helpful if children can subitize, meaning they are able to recognise a small number of items without counting. You often see this occurring when they play board games and recognise dot dice patterns without counting. Some children can also recognise the number of fingers held up without needing to count them. When children are counting up, encourage them to continue to count up from the number of items they can subitize without starting the count from one.

Addition situations are often simple to demonstrate practically. However, some children are unsure even when they do an activity with real objects whether their total

Providing lots of opportunities for calculating using natural objects

Essential addition vocabulary

Add	Plus
Total	Not enough
Altogether	The same as
One more	Equal
Count up	Add together
Number line	

number will be larger or smaller than the number they started with. It is important that all children have lots of opportunities to develop their understanding of addition through practical activities and discussion. In more formal addition situations it is always more efficient to add by starting with the largest set or number.

Many researchers have found that if the formal addition sign is introduced before young children have had the opportunity to explore different ways of solving addition problems, it can prevent them from investigating addition and recording those investigations in a range of ways. Supporting children in their own mark-making and recording usually helps them become more creative in their mathematical thinking. You can also approach addition through situations such as giving children five objects and asking them to suggest ways of sorting those objects into two sets. They can then count the number of objects in each set and record in their own way how many there are altogether.

Reading or telling the children stories which involve a focus on adding is another way of developing children's knowledge of addition. This is particularly true if you encourage them to act out the stories. At story time, with the help of puppets, develop a group story involving an adding situation. This could be where a character has to add together how many of his friends are coming to tea, e.g. the two squirrels and the three rabbits, or how many biscuits there are altogether if there are one chocolate and two ginger biscuits. Support children to learn rhymes or songs involving adding and demonstrate how they can use their fingers to make a total.

Adding — experiences and activities

Marble counting

Children can spend a long time playing with the following piece of equipment and you will find that they can have very in-depth conversations with you about number combinations and number bonds.

You need a small plastic tray or shallow straight-sided dish. Divide the dish into two areas by attaching a small length of card with sticky tape across almost the whole length of the diameter of the dish. Leave a small gap at the edge with enough space for a marble to roll through. Put four marbles in the dish and encourage children to tip the dish backwards and forwards so that the marbles roll through the gap, with some marbles on one side of the card divider and some on the other. Challenge the children to find out how many different number combinations of marbles they can make. Extend the activity by increasing the number of marbles in the dish.

Add-a-domino game

You need:

- a set of dominoes face down on the table

- numeral cards (0-12) or wooden numerals.

Play this game in a small group. Children take it in turns to pick up a domino and count how many spots there are on the domino altogether. They then select the numeral that matches their spot total. When the children are all holding a numeral they discuss what number totals they calculated. Extend the activity by offering a brick to whoever had the highest or the lowest number of domino spots and after five rounds compare the number of bricks the children have collected.

Dockyard boats

Polystyrene packing is very useful for making a floating dock in the water tray. Use a large U-shaped piece to divide the water tray into two areas, making sure that there is a space at one side of the dock for boats to sail through. Float ten plastic boats in the water and provide hand-held fans to move the boats between docks. Discuss how many boats are in the first dock, how many in the second dock and how many altogether.

Farmyard game

You need:

- a large counter or coin with one spot drawn on one side and two spots on the other

- one piece of green felt to be a field and one piece of sandpaper or brown card to represent a farmyard

- a basket containing a collection of at least ten farm animals.

Children play this game in pairs. They share the field and the farmyard. They take it in turns to toss the counter and pick up that many animals from the basket. They then decide whether to put the animals they have chosen in the farmyard or the field. Children keep taking turns until the field and the farmyard have at least three animals each or the animals are all used up. Encourage the children to count how many animals are in the farmyard or the field every time they add some more. Extend the game by increasing the number of animals used and providing a 1–3 dice instead of the counter.

Egg box addition

You need:

- two egg boxes
- a 1–6 dice
- twelve play eggs or eggs made from Plasticine
- four small pieces of card
- a number line for reference.

The children play this game in pairs, taking it in turns to throw the dice and put that many eggs in their egg box. They count and agree how many eggs they have altogether in both boxes and write the total on a card. They put their eggs back in the bowl and play again. They play four rounds and then compare the number totals they have written on their four cards with another pair of children.

The three-throws game

You need:

- a dice labelled 1,2,3,1,2,3
- a set of small world characters in a basket.

The children play this game in a small group. They take it in turns to throw the dice and collect that many characters from the basket. When everyone in the group has had three turns they each line up the characters they have collected and count how many they have altogether. While the children are playing emphasize the words add, altogether and total.

And-one-more game

You need:

- six soft toys in a hoop
- a teddy
- seven small carpet tiles arranged in a line
- a large 1-6 dice.

Children take it in turns to toss the dice, take that number of toys out of the hoop and put each toy on a carpet tile. They then add the teddy to the line of toys and say how many toys in total are in the line. Children then recount to find out the final total and say whether they guessed correctly. The toys are returned to the hoop, and the next child throws the dice and continues the game.

Hopping along game

You need:

- a numbered track with ten spaces
- six frogs numbered 1–6
- a 1–6 dice
- two pieces of shaped green card with 'lily pad' written on each.

This game is very good for supporting children who need additional practise at jumping along a number track. Ask the children to put a lily pad at the start of the track and arrange the six frogs on it. Put the second lily pad at the other end of the track next to the number 10. Children take it in turns to roll the dice and move that frog representing that number one space along the track. Talk to the children about counting on one and draw their attention to the numbers on the track. The frog winner is the one that reaches the second lily pad first. Play this game several times using different small world characters, e.g. using small cars with number stickers on them. Move the cars from one garage (small box) down the track to another garage. Extend the game by jumping backwards along the track.

Subtracting

There are three different aspects to subtraction that young learners will meet in the early years. First there is the physical removal of objects from a group (the 'take away' aspect); second the more difficult scenario of subtraction as 'counting back'; finally, the aspect that many children struggle to understand – subtraction seen as 'find the difference'.

The 'take away' scenario is the one that children find easiest to understand as they can actually take away the number of objects from a set and then count the remaining objects to find out how many are left. You will however, find that some children take a while to recognise that removing some objects from a group will make the total number decrease in size. They will need a lot of experience of taking away and discussion opportunities, sometimes just focussing on using words such as more and fewer.

Subtracting by counting back with the support of fingers or a number line is a more complex operation. Although it often involves taking away one at a time it does mean the child has to continually keep count of how many they have taken away as well as how many are left. Using equipment (e.g. Numicon plates or Multilink cube shapes) to look at the sequence of numbers that occurs when you count back from five to one helps children by providing a visual picture of how the numbers are decreasing. Using a number line to count back from one number to a smaller number is equally useful.

The most complex subtraction for young children is comparison and finding the difference. Here, children need to compare two different sets of objects to decide which has the most or the fewest. Children can often identify the set with the most but the difficulty is in identifying the number difference between the two sets. Useful experiences here include using sets of objects, putting them into two groups, and discussing and matching the two groups to find the difference. Preferably, this will be done by lining up the two groups and again using a number line to support the counting. Take the opportunity during the day to emphasize difference, e.g. when aprons and children need to be counted and paired, or

Essential subtraction vocabulary	
Take away	How many are left
Subtract	Too many
Difference	Fewer than
Count back	The same as
Total	

comparing the number of children having a packed lunch with those who are not.

Look for situations where you can highlight and link subtraction to everyday experiences and activities as they occur, such as the countdown to an exciting event or outing ('Only three days and then we go to the farm'). The children could help make a countdown poster or number line. Encourage games that involve rocket-like countdowns (5, 4, 3, 2, 1). Sing and act out number rhymes where the rhyme involves taking away each time. Playing games that involve children getting into different sized groups are also helpful for talking about comparison and difference.

Learning about taking-away by singing the five little aliens song

Subtracting — experiences and activities

The Great Rice give-away game

You need:

- two bowls each containing 500g of rice

- a small yoghurt pot for both children

- three each of the numerals 1, 2 and 3 in a bag.

Playing this game in pairs, children take it in turns to take a numeral from the bag and say its name. They then pour that number of yoghurt-pot scoopfuls of rice into the other child's bowl and return the numeral to the bag. Encourage the children to use words such as more and less to describe how much rice they have in their bowl or have given away. The game finishes when one child has collected all or most of the rice.

Bus route

Set up a small circular road system by chalking in the outdoor area or using strips of card indoors. Distribute bus stops along the road circuit. Provide two small boxes to use as minibuses, labelled 'this bus takes a maximum of ten'. Arrange 20 small world people, some at a bus stop and some on the buses. You could model driving a bus along the road system letting some toys on and off the bus. Encourage the children to join in the play, drawing their attention to the signs on the buses. Ask questions such as 'how many are on the bus now so how many toys got off?' When possible do a running commentary about the journey of the buses using the vocabulary of subtraction and emphasizing the difference between the number of toys who got on and off the bus. Extend the activity and turn it into a game by throwing two dice at each bus stop to decide how many people can get off and how many can get on the bus.

Dinosaur takeaway

You need:

- twenty dinosaurs or other counting materials for each pair

- a 1–6 dice

- a 1–20 number line.

Children play this game in pairs using a number line to support their counting backwards from 20. First, children line up and count the dinosaurs to make sure that there are 20 in the line. They then take it in turns to roll the dice and remove that many dinosaurs from the line. They recount to find how many dinosaurs are left in the line and circle that number on their number line. The children continue playing until there are no dinosaurs left in the line. Discuss with the children the numbers that they have circled. Extend the activity by providing post-it notes on which children can write their circled line numbers and compare them with other children who played the game.

Playing with a dice to add and take-away dinosaurs.

Missing bears

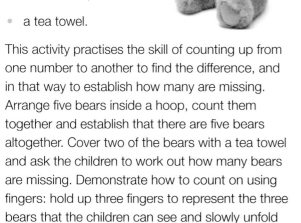

You need:

- five soft toy bears
- a small hoop
- a tea towel.

This activity practises the skill of counting up from one number to another to find the difference, and in that way to establish how many are missing. Arrange five bears inside a hoop, count them together and establish that there are five bears altogether. Cover two of the bears with a tea towel and ask the children to work out how many bears are missing. Demonstrate how to count on using fingers: hold up three fingers to represent the three bears that the children can see and slowly unfold the other two fingers to represent the missing bears. Continue the activity by having different numbers of bears missing and inviting the children to hide the bears.

What's my number?

You need:

- a chalked number track to 5
- some 'secret' numeral cards numbered 1, 2 and 3.

On the number track in the outdoor area ask one of the children to stand on number five. Explain to the other children that you are going to give her a card with a secret number on and she is going to jump back that many spaces along the track. When she has finished jumping they are to show with their fingers what number they think is on her card. When they children have finished guessing, discuss how they knew and summarize by saying, for instance, '5 jump back 2 is 3'. Continue the activity by asking other children to choose a number to stand on and giving them a secret number card. Extend the activity by using a number track to ten.

Take-away one box

You need:

- a small box
- a selection of ten different objects.

Very publicly count three objects into the box and say what they are. Count them aloud and make statements such as 'that's three altogether'. Tell the children you are going to take one item out and ask them to show how many are left in the box using their fingers. Extend the activity by encouraging the children to take it in turns to decide how many animals to put in the box and which animal to remove.

Who has more and who has fewer?

You need:

- a collection of conkers in a bag
- some counters
- ten small cards shuffled and placed face down in a pile: five cards should say 'more'; the other five cards 'fewer'.

This activity is played in pairs with children deciding has who has more and who has fewer conkers in their hand. This game is very popular with children in reception classes, who particularly enjoy the fact that holding more conkers doesn't necessarily mean you will be the winner – this depends on the card that is turned over.

Each child takes a handful of conkers, counts how many they have and compares their count total with their partner's count total. They decide which handful has more and which handful has fewer. They then turn over the top card on the more/fewer pile and whoever has the appropriate amount wins a counter. The children return the conkers to the bag, shake it and take another handful. The pair keeps on playing until they have each won three counters.

Multiplying and dividing

Multiplication is often seen as repeated addition, but it differs from addition in that the sets of objects you are totalling are made up of the same number of items. Young children's practical experience of multiplication as counting equal groups comes when they are pairing and counting items such as gloves, socks or shoes. In this way children encounter multiplication as repeated addition and counting patterns. With gloves this would be a 2, 4, 6, 8 pattern; with legs on cats, 4, 8, 12 and so on. You can record the counting pattern as jumps on a number line, making it very visual, or use numeral cards pegged on a washing line to record the sequence of counting numbers. Counting two objects as one unit is an important multiplication skill. You can help children gain experience of this by providing opportunities to count pairs of shoes in a shoe shop role-play area, offering mittens to pair up and count how many pairs there are altogether, and to match gloves, socks and any other similar pairs of objects. You could include in these pairings objects that are dissimilar but recognised by children as being part of a pair, such as knives and forks, cups and saucers and other equipment found in the home corner or dressing-up area.

It is impossible for children to have too much practical experience of grouping objects into sets and counting how many sets there are. You can of course offer experiences of grouping into a range of numbers as and when opportunities arise ('I wonder how many wheels we need to make three cars?') or extend the grouping into fives which can be related to hands ('I wonder how many hands we need to wave to see twenty fingers?')

It is important that children see evidence of multiplication in a manner other than repeated addition – it can also be seen as an arrangement of columns and rows. You can do this by providing egg boxes and apple trays for children to fill with balls, drawing their attention to layout of the spaces in those boxes and trays.

Children usually meet division as either a sharing experience or occasionally as repeated subtraction, again related to groups. Try and set up situations where children need to share out materials – card and board games are good times to rehearse sharing by giving out the cards, dice or counters. Again in practical situations children will meet halving, often in the context of food (e.g. sharing fruit or sandwiches). Emphasize to the children that when objects or sets of items are halved it is another way of saying that you are dividing something into two pieces/ sets with both pieces/sets the same size. This will go some way towards the misconception that can arise when children hear adults say, 'You can have the biggest half'. Overall, children's understanding will be deeper if they have opportunities to practise their calculation skills in real contexts.

Essential multiplication and division vocabulary

Count	Twos, fives, tens
Sets	Part
Groups of	Whole
How many altogether?	How many more?
	Lots of
Total	
	Once, twice, three times
Share	
Half	Pair
Halve	Double

Multiplying and dividing — experiences and activities

Ten fat sausages

You need:

- ten sausages (made from pieces of tights stuffed with cotton wool and tied at each end)
- a frying pan.

Sing and act out the rhyme below, each time throwing out of the pan two sausages for children to catch. During the song encourage the children to use their fingers as sausages to count backwards, turning down their fingers and recounting after each pair of sausages are thrown out. At the end of the song throw two sausages at a time back into the pan counting in twos.

Ten fat sausages rhyme

Ten fat sausages sizzling in a pan,
One went pop another went bang
Eight fat sausages sizzling in a pan,
One went pop another went bang

Six fat sausages sizzling in a pan,
One went pop another went bang
Four fat sausages sizzling in a pan,
One went pop another went bang

Two fat sausages sizzling in a pan,
One went pop another went bang

No fat sausages sizzling in a pan,
None went pop none went bang.

Giving children daily opportunities to explore counting in twos through singing rhymes such as *Ten Fat Sausages*.

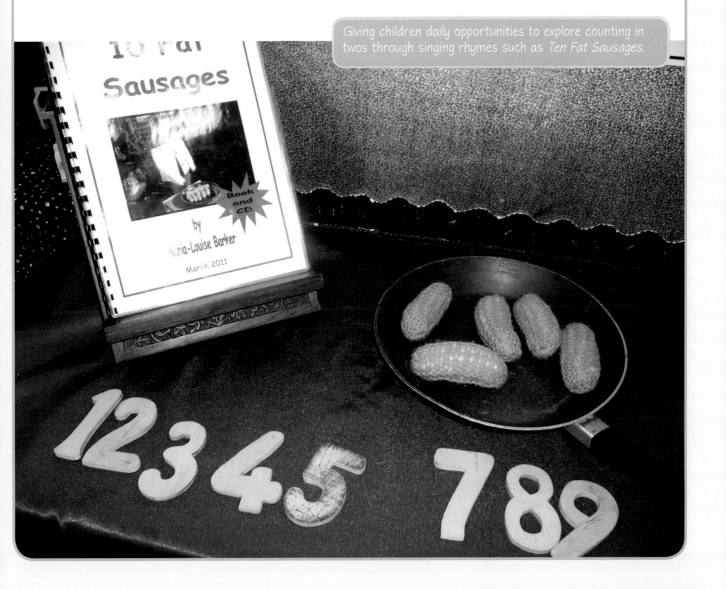

Tea party for toys

You need:

- four teddies
- four plates
- four cups
- four spoons
- eight biscuits
- sixteen pretend sandwiches.

In the role-play area set up a table and four chairs with four teddies. Ask the children to share out the food between the teddies. Encourage them to share out the items fairly between the teddies and talk about the best way to do this. Discuss together how many sandwiches each teddy has and why they each have fewer biscuits than sandwiches.

Peg up washing

Provide a selection of pairs of socks and gloves in a washing basket and encourage the children to match them up and peg them on to a washing line. When all the clothes are hanging on the line help the children to count in twos to find out how many items of clothing there are. Extend the experience by resourcing the home corner with a washing line and a selection of baby vests and tops. Supply lots of pegs (enough for two pegs for each item hung on the line) and then encourage the children to count out the pegs and place them onto each item before pegging on the line.

Money count

Resource an area with a bowl of 1p and 2p coins. Encourage the children to put the 1p coins in stacks of five and count in fives to find out how much money there is altogether. Suggest they make a stack of 2p coins big enough to make 10p. Extend the activity by using four stacks of five 1p coins un-stacked to make a long snake. Talk about how many stacks there would be if you restacked the snake in fives.

Calculator numbers

Use calculators to support children's play with numbers and their numeral recognition. You will find that the majority of calculators have the facility to count in sequence and once they are shown, most young children can recall this procedure. Use an extra large calculator to demonstrate to the children how to programme the calculator to count in different number sequences. To count in ones press (1+==) and continue slowly pressing the equals button so that the children can see the number sequence changing. After a couple of presses make statements such as 'I wonder what the next number will be'. To count in twos press (2+==), to count in fives press (5+==) and so on.

Doubling dominoes

You need:

- a large collection of small world toys, counters, cubes, paper clips and other small objects in a box

- the 1–5 doubles from a domino set in a small bag

- some paper plates, one per player.

Play this game in a small group. First, give each child a paper plate to keep their collection on. Explain that they should take it in turns to choose a domino from the bag. They count the number of spots on one side of the domino and double it. To check they count all the spots on the domino. They return the domino to the bag and then count out that number of objects from the box to put on their plate. Their plate is full when they have more than twenty objects on it. You can make the game more challenging by doubling each domino double total.

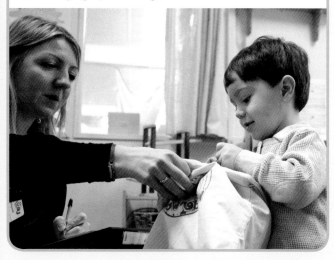

Children can explore calculating using natural objects outdoors.

Penny arrays game

You need:

- a 3x3 grid

- fifteen 1p coins for each player

- a 1–3 dice.

Children take it in turns to roll the dice and pick up that many coins. They put out the coins they have picked up on their own grid, one penny in each square. When they have filled their own grid they can offer any leftover coins to another player.

Muffin tins game

You need:

- a muffin tray with a paper fairy-cake case in each space

- a large box of buttons

- a 1–6 dice.

Children take it in turns to throw the dice and put that many buttons in the tin. They may either put all their buttons in one case or share them out between the cases. When all the cases contain five buttons the game is over and the children can then count in fives to find out how many buttons they have used altogether. Extend the game by collecting ten buttons in each case and counting in tens at the end of the game.

The role of the adult

In an environment that is rich in calculating experiences you should be able to observe children while they are playing, calculating and comparing quantities as well as during the daily routines that occur. There should be opportunities to see them engaged in the following:

- **Using and understanding the language of calculation such as altogether, more and fewer.**

- **Counting to find out the total number of objects in two groups and making sensible estimates of the total.**

- **Comparing amounts in two sets and saying which is more or fewer.**

- **Recording using objects or marks they can interpret and explain.**

Enriching provision

- **Provide collections of objects to sort, count, compare and rearrange.**

- **In discussion and talk, use the vocabulary of calculation.**

- **In practical activities, introduce experiences of calculation.**

- **Display a variety of number lines at child height.**

- **Sing together and use equipment to illustrate the calculation potential in nursery rhymes and finger play.**

- **In the maths area put out some dice, spinners, number cards and number tracks with a selection of small world characters as well as counters, and have a maths-game session.**

Book corner

Audit the books in your book corner to check that you have books that show counting forward as well as backward. Resource with stories that contain an element of calculation.

Extend the activities in your story sacks by including a dice game and number track as well as a calculating activity.

Music area

Use different instruments to play groups of sounds and make up a twelve-beat score such as three beats on the triangle, three beats on the drum, three beats on the cymbal, three beats on the xylophone. Invite the children to write a poster of the music score.

Encourage the children to invent clapping rhythms and draw their attention to the repetition of the groups of sound patterns.

Outdoor area

Provide numbered sand buckets in two different colours – ask children to collect the correct number of twigs in each bucket, then order them in a 'red, green, red, green' line so that the pattern of twos is emphasized.

Play games that involve using number tracks and a large dice.

Introduce scoring for some of the games outdoors and provide chalkboards to make scoring possible in ball and skittle play.

Open-ended questions and enabling statements about calculating

How can we find out how many fingers we both have altogether?

I wonder what the best way to share out the biscuits is?

It looks like there might be twenty altogether – what do you think?

I'm not sure if they all have the same number.

What shall we do first to find out if there's any missing?

How many more do we need?

I wonder if anyone has fewer than me?

Maths home challenges

Sing-a-song

Learn a number song or finger rhyme and sing it to someone. If you can't find a song, try this one about elephants.

An elephant went out to play on a spider's web one day.
(wiggle fingers about)

He thought it such tremendous fun he called for another one to come.
(show two fingers)

Elephant, elephant. (whisper)

Two elephants went out to play on a spider's web one day.
(wiggle fingers about)

They thought it such tremendous fun they called for another one to come.
(show three fingers)

Elephant, elephant. (whisper)

Keep singing until you have five elephants.

Have fun!

Money count

Look for coins at home or ask an adult if you can borrow some.

Put the coins in stacks of two and count how many stacks you have made.

Can you make four stacks with five coins in each stack?

How many coins did you use altogether?

Use a pencil and paper and make some rubbings of the coins.

Have fun!

Shoe sort

Collect some pairs of shoes and muddle them all up in a box.

Now see how fast you can put the pairs together again.

When you have finished, count how many shoes and how many pairs you put together.

Don't forget to put the shoes away when you have finished counting them.

Have fun!

Working with shapes

All children need to actively explore and experience shape, space and position in two and three dimensions as well as playing with pattern and symmetry. Fortunately our whole world consists of various different shapes and space, and with encouragement a child can spend a lot of time exploring shape and space as they run in straight lines and skip in circles, build castles, make models, create pictures, invent patterns, crawl under the table, fly high on a swing or climb on a frame.

In the early years it is important that young children handle and play with lots of different types of shapes. This helps them begin to appreciate the varying properties, not just of regular shapes but irregular ones as well. Children need to build, make patterns, print with, cut apart and put back together lots of 2D and 3D shapes so that their experiences are more than just a 'name that shape' activity. They must focus on the way 3D shapes stack, roll and pack as well as looking at how 2D shapes fit together and the spaces they leave when they don't quite fit.

You can set up activities that help children begin to appreciate which shapes are best to use for different purposes, e.g. which shape to use for wheels, which shaped bricks they need in order to build a bridge or what shapes you can make when you cut a sandwich in two pieces.

Children will, with your support, begin to know and be able to use the very specific vocabulary of shape. Ensure that children use 3D shapes for constructions and are also aware that they can open out hollow shapes such as boxes to reveal a 2D shape. The experiences you offer children should give them the opportunity to describe and discuss shapes and patterns and use simple words to describe the position of objects. In this way children will be able to use and recognise a variety of 2D and 3D shapes in lots of different situations.

The emphasis in the activities and experiences you provide for shape and space should be on children's own observations as they handle, build, paint and work with a variety of 2D and 3D shapes. Although here, the different learning aspects of shape and space have been separated, you will find that many of them overlap naturally as you are playing and working with the children. Refer to the way different bricks stack or fit together and on some occasions provide a commentary on what children are doing, e.g. 'That looks good the way you've balanced that cylinder on the top of the tower'.

Identifying shapes

When children are working with 2D and 3D shapes they may sometimes want to know the name of a particular shape. Although drawing their attention to the properties of that shape is important, there are occasions when also giving them the relevant shape name or the vocabulary linked to that shape is appropriate.

Shapes with three dimensions are classified according to how many faces the shape has:

Number of faces	Shape name
1	sphere or ovoid
4	tetrahedron
5	pentahedron
6	hexahedron
7	septahedron
8	octahedron
9	nonahedron
10	decahedron
11	undecahedron
12	dodecahedron
20	icosahedron

Shapes with two dimensions that is width and height and are closed are classified according to how many sides the shape has:

Number of sides	Shape name
1	circle or oval
3	triangle
4	quadrilateral

(included in this group are square, rectangle and rhombus)

Number of sides	Shape name
5	pentagon
6	hexagon
8	octagon
10	decagon

Recycled materials offer engaging opportunities to explore 3D shapes.

3D shapes

A 3D shape has three dimensions. In other words, you can take three measurements of the shape: its height, its width and its depth. The important aspect of any 3D shape to consider is how many faces and edges the shape has and whether or not those edges and faces are all the same shape and size. If so, the shape will be classified as a 'regular' shape like a cube. Alternatively, if the shape has edges that are different lengths or faces that are different shapes that shape will be called an 'irregular' 3D shape. It is important to recognise whether a shape is regular or irregular as it affects the construction potential of the shape. For example, a regular tetrahedron (another name for a triangle-based pyramid) will be easier to build with than an irregular pyramid.

There are some 3D shapes, such as a sliced loaf or a cylinder, that when cut through, always give slices of the same shape and size. This is true no matter how many slices you cut, and these shapes are known as prisms.

Children need lots of experience of making models by putting together and taking apart pieces from construction sets to discover and understand the properties of different 3D shapes. They will benefit from a range of play experiences that involve stacking, balancing and building with 3D shapes including play with recycled materials. Encourage them to build tall towers and large models using junk boxes, and provide plastic blocks of different sizes so that they can make walls, stairs and bridges. It is particularly important that you discuss 3D shape with children as they build and construct different things. Encourage them to try out different shapes and decide which one is best for that purpose. Discuss what would happen if they changed, rearranged and later deconstructed those models. Most children use trial and error methods when they are building models – ensure that you support their efforts with statements such as 'I wonder what will happen if you turn that brick sideways'.

Talk through the decisions children make as they are tidying away, putting things on shelves and sorting into boxes. You will need to make sure that they use 3D shapes made in a variety of materials and colours so that they do not assume that only red wooden shapes can be called cubes. Use mathematical shape vocabulary with the children as well as accepting their descriptions of the properties and probably the invented names that they give any 3D shapes they are working with.

Essential 3D-shape vocabulary	
Solid shape	Sphere or ovoid
Hollow shape	Edge
Cube	Corner
Cuboid	Face
Pyramid	Same
Cylinder	Different

Initially many children confuse the name of the 3D shape and the 2D face of the shape, for example when building with cube wooden bricks they may refer to them as squares, or on occasion the other way round. Offer the correct shape name by using it when you summarize and extend what the children have said, for example 'Yes I like building with cubes. I think they're very good for constructing towers'.

Any recording of 3D constructions can be done by taking photographs and enlarging them as well as or instead of sketches and plans. If the construction is moveable you can also use a photocopier to show a sideways view or outline. Lay the construction on the glass photocopier plate and cover it with a piece of material. Press print and you should get a fairly clear image.

Children can explore shapes using dough.

3D shapes — experiences and activities

Housing giants

You need:

- two very large cardboard boxes
- wallpaper
- paste
- bubblewrap
- scissors
- Stanley knife.

1. Build a house outdoors for a giant, should one ever come to visit. Construct on a huge scale – you could use large boxes from refrigerator or other white-goods packaging.

2. Discuss with the children ways to attach the boxes to each other. Cut out a door and windows and draw a cross on the face of the box which will be the base of the house and therefore in contact with the ground. When you are talking with the children use shape words such as faces, edges, hollow and cuboid.

3. Cut down two edges of each box so that you can flatten them; this is an ideal time to draw children's attention to what a cuboid looks like when you open it out and talk about the 2D shapes they can see. Paste wallpaper onto the printed faces of the 'outside' of the box except for the face with the cross and the spaces that will be the window and door.

4. Now turnover the box so that the plain 'inside' of the original box is uppermost. Paste bubble wrap onto five of the faces of the box, again leaving out the base and the spaces for the window and door.

5. Reassemble the box using masking tape to stick together the cut edges, with the wallpapered faces on the inside and the bubble wrap on the outside.

6. When the box is assembled children can paint the bubble wrap and play in the house until the giant arrives. Use group time to reflect on how the giant's house was made.

Build a bear

This activity will provide children with the opportunity to use words describing 3D and 2D shapes. Read a story where a bear is the central character, for example *Where's my Teddy?* by Jez Alborough (Walker Books, 2004). Provide the children with a collection of recycled boxes, tubes and other materials and explain that together they are going to build a bear. Encourage the children to sort out the boxes before they start building and discuss how the boxes fit together. They should think about which shapes would be good to use for the bear's head and which they could use for the arms and legs. After they have worked together on making a large bear some children may want to go on to make their own individual bears using small recycled boxes or make a 2D version using collage materials.

Using a made lotto game made with photos of different shaped objects, taken by the children.

Sandscapes

In this activity children will need access to a supply of damp sand, preferably outdoors. If you don't have an outdoor sandpit you can fill a redundant inflatable paddling pool with sand or put down a tarpaulin and tip some sand onto it. Remember that you will need to cover the sand at the end of the session. Provide a range of plastic containers that are different shapes and sizes as well as digging implements such as small sand shovels. Show the children how to fill up a container to the top and level it out using the spade before carefully tipping it out to make a sand pie. Challenge them to cover the whole surface of the sandpit with sand pies. When the children have made lots of different shaped and sized pies, establish with them which container made which pie. Draw attention to and make comments on the features of the sand pies, e.g. 'I like the tall shape you've made with the square top'; 'I think you used this bucket to make that sand pie – I can see that it is a much wider shape at one end just like the bucket.' To extend the activity set up an interactive display outdoors: make a line of three differently-shaped sand pies on a flat surface, then ask the children to choose a sand pie and guess which container it was made in.

Threading shapes

Collect together small recycled boxes such as individual-sized cereal packets and cheese boxes. Using a hole punch make a hole on two different faces of the box, then with a tapestry or plastic needle and embroidery thread show the children how to thread the boxes into long lines. Suspend the boxes on a washing line. Children could paint the boxes before threading, and are provided with a better surface for painting if they turn the boxes inside out beforehand. They can do this by cutting along two sides of a box (a long edge and an adjacent short edge) to reveal the 2D net of the shape and then reassembling the box with the printed side now inside the box. They will need to use masking tape to stick together the two cut edges.

Impressions

Resource a sand tray containing fairly damp sand with 3D shapes, and encourage the children to make impressions in the sand. Make handprints, footprints and use large pebbles to make indentations. Use a variety of irregular shapes to make prints in the sand and support the children in experimenting to find out which type of shape makes the best imprints.

What's inside?

You need:

- a roll of tin foil

- three fairly large toy objects with defined features e.g. a bus, a telephone and a saucepan.

Unknown to the children, choose one of the toys to wrap in tin foil and then carefully remove the foil so that it keeps the shape of the particular object. Show the children the three toys and talk about the various features of each object, for example 'This saucepan has a round base and a long handle'. 'Can you see the small square windows on this bus?' When children have looked at and handled the objects, show them the tin foil shape and ask them to suggest which of the objects was wrapped inside it. If the children can identify which object it was but not verbalize why, support them in trying to explain how they knew which object it was by offering comments such as 'I expect you knew that it was the telephone because you saw the circle shape of the dial'.

Extend the activity by wrapping a different object and then removing it from the wrapping. Give all the children a figure from a small world collection and ask them to put their figure by the object that they think made the shape in the foil. When everyone has 'voted' by placing their figure, count how many figures are beside each object and talk about how many votes each object has. At this point, identify a shape feature from each object and then reveal which object had been wrapped in the foil.

2D shapes

The 2D shapes that young children work with most are mostly circles and polygons. A polygon is a two-dimensional shape constructed of straight lines that all join up so that the shape is closed. Polygons have different names depending on how many sides they have, so a four-sided polygon is a quadrilateral. The quadrilateral group is then further divided into squares, rectangles and rhombus, depending on whether all sides are the same length, whether the sides are parallel and whether the angles are all the same size.

Fortunately young children don't need to learn all the polygon shape names and variations in the quadrilateral group. They may be interested to know though that if they ever see a shape with a million sides it is called a Megagon.

Children in the early years need hands-on experience of a wide range of different sized 2D shapes, both regular and irregular. This is especially relevant with triangles as children often assume that an equilateral triangle (a triangle with sides of the same length and angles of equal sizes) is the only 'real' triangle and that any other three-sided shape is not a triangle but something else. Many children also go through a stage where they will only acknowledge a triangle as such if it is sitting firmly on its base, point upwards. A triangle in any other orientation

Essential 2D-shape vocabulary	
Flat shape	Rectangle
Circle	Hexagon
Triangle	Side
Square	Corner

is regarded suspiciously as another shape rather than a triangle. The same misconception in young children occurs with their view of a square, in that they often regard any square set at an angle as definitely not a square.

When focusing on 2D shapes children will benefit enormously from making patterns, pictures and designs using 2D shapes. Designs can be made using a variety of materials: perhaps a collection of different shapes made from the same material such as felt, sticky paper or newspaper from which children make a picture using a range of shapes. Alternatively you can provide the same shape in lots of different sizes and in the same material. Provide tissue paper shapes and encourage the children to glue them overlapping each other, then to look and see whether they have made other 2D shapes in the overlaps.

When children are using 2D shapes to print, a running commentary from you will focus their attention on what is happening in their design rather than randomly printing. Identify for them when they are using the same shape in different positions and orientations.

Look for shapes in the outdoor environment and point them out by playing 'I spy shapes'. Children can make mobiles and wind chimes to hang outdoors, for example by threading straws onto thin elastic and then tying it to make a triangle. The important thing is to draw children's attention to the shape instead of the intricacies of threading by making statements such as 'I wonder how many straws we will need to make a square?'. To familiarize children with a range of different 2D shapes you will need to make sure that there are 'posting' shape boxes available for children to play with and jigsaw picture trays where children can remove and put back the shapes.

Theo cut out his own shapes to make a happy day picture.

2D shapes — experiences and activities

Chalking and walking shapes

On a hard surface in the outdoor area use playground chalks to draw large 2D shapes. Encourage the children to walk round the shape using small steps then long strides, then to hop or skip around the shape. Children could try drawing their own shapes to walk round. As they are drawing make comments such as 'I wonder if you're drawing a shape with three corners?' or 'It looks like you're drawing a circle'. You could change the activity by using skipping ropes laid on the ground to make the shapes, or ribbons and scarves to draw the shapes in the air. Extend the activity by drawing shapes on an indoor table and suggesting children choose a small world figure to walk along the sides of the shape. They could also line up cars, dinosaurs or other small world characters along the sides of drawn, 2D card or plastic shapes.

Torchlight

You need:

- some plastic 2D shapes
- scissors,
- A4 paper
- pencils
- a hole punch
- small torches.

Ask the children to choose a shape, position it in the middle of a piece of A4 paper and draw round the sides of the shape. Depending on dexterity they may need help with both this and the following step, which is to use a hole punch to punch holes along the drawn outline. Show the children how to shine the torchlight through the holes so that the shape image is reflected on a wall. Extend the activity by inviting children to draw, hole punch and reflect their own patterns.

Hide-and-seek squares

You need:

- a collection of assorted squares of different sizes, colours and materials (e.g. plastic, card or felt).

This activity focuses on the properties of a square. Hide the squares in a small area making sure that they are all accessible to the children. You can make it more difficult by hiding some squares underneath other objects but make sure that children who are often easily discouraged can find some squares quite quickly. When the children have found some squares discuss together the differences between them (i.e. the different sizes, colours and material). Establish that all the shapes the children have found are squares because each has four corners and sides of the same length. You can extend the activity the following day by announcing that some other shapes have fallen into the squares box and asking for volunteers to sort them out. Extend the activity even further by giving each child a pair of the same shape – they must hide one shape from their pair and swap their remaining shape with someone else. Then they search for the matching pair of their new shape.

A missing shape

Arrange two different 2D shapes on a tray together with a couple of small world toys. Discuss all the objects on the tray, including shape words where relevant. Secretly remove one of the shapes and ask the children to identify what's missing. If they can only identify the name of the shape use statements or questions such as 'Mmm is that the shape with three corners?' If you remove one of the other objects ask the children to say something about it rather than simply naming the object.

Side-to-side rollers

You need:

- a roll of masking tape
- paper
- paints
- paint rollers.

This painting activity will produce 2D shapes with a very strong image and emphasizes the number of sides on different shapes. Show the children how to cut different lengths of masking tape and stick them onto a piece of paper to create a closed shape. Make sure the ends of each length of masking tape overlap at the corners of the shape. Three different lengths can be arranged to make a triangle. Four pieces can make a square or a rectangle or another type of quadrilateral. As long as the ends of the masking tape all touch the children can create any sided shape they wish. The children finish sticking down the masking tape to make their shape and then roller over it with a paint roller dipped in paint. Make sure that they cover the entire paper including the inside and outside of the shape. When the paint is dry remove the masking tape to reveal the shape. Instead of creating shapes, younger children may use the tape to create lines and crossing points – this is fine.

Smorgasbord

You need:

- a sliced loaf of bread that has been lightly toasted
- a choice of fillings such as soft cheese, egg mayonnaise and hummus
- different shaped biscuit cutters and knives
- small slices of a vegetable such as cucumber to decorate.

Suggest the children choose a cutter and then cut as many of that shape from a slice of toast as they can. They then spread a filling onto each shape and decorate it if they wish using slices of vegetables. When all the toast has been used discuss which fillings are on the different shapes. Then eat and enjoy!

Biscuits to go

Involve the children in mixing, rolling and cutting out the following biscuit recipe and wrap each biscuit in a square of tissue for the children to take home. This recipe makes 25–30 biscuits.

You need:

- biscuit cutters
- rolling pins
- baking tray
- a skewer for writing the child's initial.

Ingredients:

- 300g plain flour
- 250g softened butter or margarine
- 125g caster sugar
- 1 egg yolk
- 1 tsp vanilla essence

Step 1:
Mix the butter and sugar together, add the egg yolk and stir in the flour to form a dough.

Step 2:
Add a couple of teaspoons of water only if the dough is very dry.

Step 3:
Roll out the dough to about 2cm deep and use the cutters to press out the biscuit shapes.

Step 4:
Let children use a skewer to write the first letter of their name on their biscuits.

Step 5:
Put the biscuits on a greased baking tray and cook at 160 degrees/gas mark 4 for 15 minutes.

Position, direction and movement

This section is about supporting children in understanding the 'space element' of the shape and space curriculum. Children should become familiar with words that are used to indicate where they are, and their position in relation to others. This does not mean only positional words/phrases such as next to and in front of but also directional words that describe routes, movement and journeys; children need to be confident in using all of these. They need the opportunity to observe places and things from different viewpoints and to explore how things work, how objects fit together and how their whole body coordinates and uses space and balance.

The kind of experiences that children should have when they are learning about position, movement and direction are often things that they are probably doing already such as positioning small world characters in the sand. They are likely to be moving around the outdoor area on bikes, wheeling prams and chasing balls in different directions. The support they need from you takes the form of a commentary on what they are doing, supplying essential words to describe what is happening. Use questions and comments such as 'What did you see when you crawled underneath the slide?' and 'I saw you ride your bike very fast past the slide and across the grass'.

Set challenges for children to walk about the outside area in different ways, for example stretching tall, running in straight lines, in zigzags, in a large circle or making a curve with their body. Create circuits outdoors where children can move from one area to another without touching the ground. Together make an obstacle course for small cars using ramps, bridges and other construction materials. Use plastic crates upended and large plastic building blocks to make a maze for children to negotiate. Suggest they choose a friend and stand next to them, behind them and in front of them and then try doing the same thing with a teddy and a doll.

To help children learn about direction, play movement games as a group or class involving instructions such as 'take three steps backwards, one step sideways towards the hedge, two steps forward' and then decide whether you are in a different place from where you started. Gather together a group of children and play follow-my-leader: past the climbing frame, through the tunnel, over the sand pit, up the steps and down the slide. Encourage children to take it in turns to be the leader.

Organize other types of trail, such as a crumb trail, for children to follow, treasure hunts and if possible use programmable toys to draw pathways, helping children to describe the routes and directions. Chalk outlines of roads outdoors to make a network for children to follow using small cars or to walk small world people along. You could try going big with the network and creating a road system for the children to pedal or scoot along but don't forget you might need to provide pedestrian crossings.

During circle time, play a game of 'I'm thinking of a friend' and describe a particular child by the position they are sitting in. For example 'I'm thinking of a friend who is sitting between Theo and Ella', then wait for that child or others in the circle to identify them. When everyone knows the identity of the friend make sure you summarize the position 'Yes, Jack is sitting between Theo and Ella'.

Essential vocabulary of position, movement and direction

Straight line	Follow	To
Curved line	Finish	Along
Forwards	End	Above
Backwards	Under	Inside
Route	Over	Outside
Pathway	Next	Up
Start	In front of	Down
Stop	Behind	Next to
Position	Start from	Between
Arrow		

Position, direction and movement — experiences and activities

Dancing leaves

In the outdoor area encourage children to use brooms and rakes to make a pile of leaves or use cut-out paper tissue leaves inside the classroom. Take a handful of leaves each and throw them in the air; comment on the movement of the leaves and how they fall to the ground using words like spin, spiral, turn and float. Suggest to the children that they stand high up (such as on the climbing frame) and throw the leaves, then watch and describe the leaf movement they see. Enrich the activity by giving the children handheld battery-operated fans or paper fans to blow the leaves. Try showing them what happens to the leaves when you use a garden leaf-blower. You could start a leaf blowing dance together.

Looking for a straight line

Tape an un-lidded felt tip pen to the bottom edge of a closed door and slide drawing paper or newspaper underneath – when the door is opened the pen will draw a movement line on the paper. Discuss with the children what shape of line the pen will draw when the door is opened. Introduce words and phrases such as straight line, curved line, zigzag line and circle. Children are likely to suggest that the door will draw a straight line when they open it. The excitement when they watch the door open and it draws a large curve is very contagious. Children then often start to attach a range of pens to the bottom edge of the door, convinced there is a straight line to be found somewhere. Of course they continue to get curved lines of varying sizes depending where along the edge of the door they positioned the pen. You could then suggest that they look for the elusive straight line by recording how other objects move. They may try taping pens to other doors in case that particular door is different, and eventually some will attach a pen to a drawer and record a straight line as it moves. These experiments with and recordings of movement will provide an opportunity to introduce the related language.

Line squirts

You need:

- a large white sheet

- some old newspapers

- a range of different coloured runny paints in squirty bottles (empty washing-up liquid bottles work if you do not have any purpose-made bottles).

In the outdoor area, peg up on a washing line the large sheet with the newspaper underneath to catch paint drips. Encourage the children to squirt the paint onto the sheet using large arm movements and drawing straight, curved and wiggly lines.

Button and counter snakes

In the outdoor area resource a flat space with a selection of counters, buttons, small stones, conkers, small plastic bears, small world farm animals or other similar materials sorted into separate boxes and containers. Encourage the children to make snakes with different objects. You could show them how to make a spiral snake by arranging the bears or a zigzag snake with conkers.

Following the trail

Outdoors, give the children playground chalk so that they can draw a line from one area to another. Suggest they make the shortest route or 'the route that goes past the three bears' house', for example. Develop the idea by using painted lines for children to follow on scooters or bikes. You can use watered-down paint which disappears quickly when it rains. Encourage the children to make directional notices that tell you where you go if you follow the yellow lines, in a similar manner to many large department stores or train stations where you can follow different coloured lines to take you to different areas. Children may also draw maps to show the way to the hall or the outside door.

Outdoor play gives time and space to explore 3D shapes on a larger scale.

Line prints

You need:

- some thick paints and a roller

- large plastic trays or a table top and paper to print on

- a selection of small mark-making implements such as sticks, twigs and cotton wool buds.

Show the children how to cover the surface of a tray by using a roller and a spoonful of paint. Encourage the children to take their finger or a stick for a 'walk' across the painted surface, drawing curved lines. When most of the tray surface is covered with lines, press a piece of paper on it to take a print of the lines. Together, look at the print to identify the closed spaces between the lines and where lines cross. Try and follow the route of some of the lines. Extend the experience by providing plastic combs or builders' plaster combs to make line patterns across the wet surface of the paint.

Line drawing

Focus on the experience of drawing lines by tying an elastic band round a bunch of different coloured felt tip pens. Encourage the children to draw multiple lines at the same time by using the bunch of pens to draw shapes, angles, curves and zigzags over a large piece of paper.

Pattern and Symmetry

A pattern always contains elements that repeat over and over again in a predictable way. Sometimes children and even adults confuse pattern with design and will say 'look at my pattern' when what they have created is a design. In order to class something as a pattern, you must be able to see aspects of repeatability. A key element of any pattern should be a mathematical rule – when children make patterns they are learning about applying a rule even if, at the beginning, those elements of pattern are sometimes in the wrong order. An example of a simple rule is 'every other one' which could translate as a red bead, a blue bead, a red bead, a blue bead or a line consisting of an elephant, a dinosaur, an elephant, a dinosaur and so on.

Most of the early patterning experiences that children work on have a focus of shape, size or colour using real objects. It helps children's understanding of pattern if adults identify and comment on the patterns they see in their everyday world. Display material and wrapping papers that have a repeating pattern.

Identify the patterns that occur in children's daily routines, and talk about and encourage them to create their own patterns in art, music, dance and movement. Music provides a good context for identifying repeating patterns and many songs have repeated lines or choruses. Introduce clapping sequences and games or make up action patterns and link these with number patterns, e.g. two hops, one jump, two hops, one jump.

Remember that many stories have a strong repeated pattern and sequence to them, e.g. *We're Going on a Bear Hunt* by Michael Rosen (Walker Books, 1993). Draw children's attention to the pattern when you have finished the story. For any story with a repeating chorus you should occasionally say 'I wonder what's going to happen on the next page?'

Focus on texture to create patterns and introduce new vocabulary to describe the texture of different materials. Talk aloud to yourself about what you are doing while you are sitting next to a child: 'I think I'll make a pattern by using a shiny button and then that soft felt circle and then another shiny button. . .' Provide materials and resources for children to observe and describe patterns in the indoor and outdoor areas. Help them to explore patterns that they can touch and see in their environment.

It is important that you support children in recognising and indentifying the symmetrical aspects of leaves, flowers, fruit and vegetables. Use a variety of media to create symmetrical designs and make sure that children have the opportunity to look at, discuss and identify the symmetrical designs made by others. Use your outdoor area to collect environmental patterns and take photographs of flowers, spider's webs and fir cones.

Set up an outdoor art gallery where the children's pattern prints, symmetrical drawings and photographs can be displayed. Extend the gallery by providing an interactive display of artefacts that can be handled, such as fir cones and sunflower heads as well as patterns and leaf arrangements that can be added to. Use arrow notices with illustrations to show where in the outdoor area patterns can be seen, e.g. 'Look here and see the dandelions growing. Can you see any patterns?'. Provide mirror tiles so that children can reflect and identify the symmetrical patterns they find.

Essential vocabulary of pattern and symmetry

Match	Last	Smooth
Shape	Next	Soft
Same	Pattern	Hard
Different	Repeat	Shiny
First	Fold	Dull
Second	Rough	Copy

Pattern and symmetry — experiences and activities

Making sounds and music

Make sound patterns using musical instruments; try making a pattern using two instruments, for example, bang the drum, bang the triangle, bang the drum and so on. Use one instrument and bang once, then give two fast beats. Make a loud noise, a soft noise etc. Try clapping rhythms to music or nursery rhymes.

Giant weaving

In the outdoor area use a mixture of ribbons, thick wool and skipping ropes to weave giant patterns using either the fence or some bamboo sticks fixed into the ground. Cut up plastic supermarket bags into strips and plait them using two strips and the 'under, over, under, over' technique. Children can then weave these strips into the giant weaving patterns.

Mirrors

Hinge together with masking tape pairs of small plastic mirrors. Stand the mirrors upright and in the angle where the two mirrors meet place a small world figure such as a dinosaur or frog. Show the children how to slowly open the mirrors and look at the reflections they can see as the angle on the mirror widens. Leave a collection of different figures for the children to experiment with as they open and close the mirrors. You could draw their attention to the number of figures they can see in the mirrors.

Celebration bunting

Make chains or bunting for the outdoor area using triangles cut from material or coloured paper. Use two or three different colours and create a repeating pattern. Staple the triangles onto long pieces of tape and suspend them low enough for children to be able to touch them and rehearse the pattern. Use other shapes to make more bunting or use two types of materials.

Printing a veggie pattern

Explore pattern through printing with vegetables. In the creative area, place rollers, sponges and paints and a selection of vegetables such as potatoes, carrots and broccoli. Cut all the vegetables into halves, quarters and slices. Encourage the children to experiment with making patterns using different vegetables. Extend the activity by providing narrow strips of paper and printing repeating patterns to make long vegetable streamers.

Lots of shapes to talk about and discuss in the minibeast hotel.

Double dominoes

Show the children a double five domino from a set of large dominoes. Count the dots together and discuss the 'sameness' of five on each half of the domino. Help the children to search for other dominoes that have the same number of spots on each half. Extend the activity by providing six rectangular pieces of thin card and stickers for each child so that they can make their own set of double dominoes.

Name patterns

Use alphabet letters either cut from magazines or newspaper headlines, or allow children to cut their own letters from these. Use the letters or even whole words to make repeating patterns. Children could also make patterns by changing the orientation of the letter they have chosen, for example, the letter A the right way up, then upside down, then the right way up, and so on. Change the activity by choosing numbers to make a pattern; write the numeral large then small, then large, then small etc. Ask questions such as 'What's the same? What's different about them?'

Silhouette symmetry

Use a reading lamp, large torch or even an overhead projector to reflect outlines of symmetrical objects on a wall. Challenge children to guess what the object is and support their guesses by describing the shape of the object. You could pin paper on the wall, draw round the shadow and cut it out so that you have a record of the shapes. Annotate each of the shapes with the children's suggestions of what it was, identifying the symmetry.

Pizza patterns

You need:

- plain pizza bases

- tomato puree and grated cheese

- a selection of toppings such as cherry tomatoes, mushrooms, sliced peppers, sliced sausages and basil leaves

- knives or spreaders.

Show the children how to spread the tomato puree over the pizza base then make a pattern round the edge of the pizza using different toppings. Other patterns can be made across the centre of the pizza base. Cook according to the pizza-base recipe instructions and enjoy!

Exploring 2D shapes and repeating patterns in the creative workshop.

The role of the adult

These experiences and activities are particularly valuable for helping children understand shape and space:

- **playing with shapes and fitting shapes together**

- **using construction sets and making models from junk materials**

- **doing simple jigsaws and using shape-posting boxes**

- **tidying up, packing things away and fitting things in boxes**

- **identifying and creating patterns and symmetrical pictures in a range of media**

- **inventing and describing movements by turning their body in different ways**

- **identifying symmetry in natural objects and drawing children's attention to it**

- **experiencing and learning about the properties of 2D and 3D shapes**

Building with blocks outdoors.

Enriching provision

Enriching provision with selected mathematical shape and space materials encourages children to integrate purposeful thinking about maths ideas as well as drawing and building maths into their play. Include materials such as paper tubes and empty packaging materials, large cardboard boxes, a variety of sizes of nuts and bolts for children to match and then screw pairs together on a tray in the construction area. Help children to use positional language and set up experiences of direction and position. Look for opportunities for children to recall and reflect on experiences and actions.

Engage with children in imaginative play and design, adapt or make props to support that play. Supply artefacts linked to shape and space and support children's building of symmetrical structures. Talk about what sort of shape might fit best in a space or ask what shape would definitely not fit in the space. Extend children's thinking by asking open questions that begin 'Have you thought about..?'

Provide children with regular occasions to use and explore both regular and irregular 2D shapes. Create opportunities for the children to explain what they are thinking about and how the shapes fit together. Materials can also change shape by rolling, twisting or stretching (dough for example). Use snack time as an opportunity to explore shape by cutting fruit into different shapes.

Support children in exploring, developing and clarifying their ideas about shape and space by talking about what they have been involved in and describing experiences with shapes. Ask children to suggest reasons for what happened, e.g. why their tower collapsed and encourage them to think about how they could do things differently.

Use builders' tuff spot trays for small world play. Provide stones, pieces of wood, twigs and gravel for children to create their own landscapes. Talk about pathways and routes to connect the different areas.

Collect a good supply of natural materials and encourage the children to make patterns with them. You could lay down some paving slabs or wooden patio squares for the children to use as background, or if they are working indoors provide plastic mirror tiles or light boxes for them to use to display their patterns.

Natural objects are an essential part of exploring 3D shapes.

In the construction area, play alongside children and talk about why and how they are connecting the different shapes to make a bridge, tunnel or building.

In the outdoor area use twigs, stones or shells to create line or grid patterns. Use gravel to make patterns and CD disks to reflect those patterns. Construct wind chimes by attaching different materials and objects in a repeating pattern to lengths of string.

In the role-play area introduce suitcases, boxes and bags and explore the idea of packing things into the containers for holidays, picnics or outings.

In the creative area make a 'lift the flap' display or use recycled boxes to make a peephole for children to look through and see a pattern. Put out a collection of boxes, tins and containers with lids and ask children to make sure that each has the right lid.

Open-ended questions and enabling statements about shape and space

Maths home challenges

Making sandwiches

1. First make a sandwich with two slices of bread and whatever filling you like best.

2. Cut the sandwich into two rectangles.

3. Now cut the rectangles into four squares.

4. Cut each square into two triangles.

5. How many triangles do you have altogether? Now eat all the triangles.

6. Make another sandwich and cut it into different shapes.

Have fun!

Making patterns

Collect together some mugs, plates, forks and spoons from the kitchen.

Choose eight objects from your collection – four of each type, e.g. four spoons and four plates.

Try arranging your objects to make a pattern. When you have finished take a photo of your pattern.

Can you choose another eight objects from your collection and make another pattern?

Have fun!

Making maps

Draw an outline map of the road where you live.

Show where on the map you live and mark some other things in your road such as a postbox, a lamp post or tree, or where your friend lives.

Explain your map to someone you know.

Have fun!

Learning to measure

Finding out about measures on a large scale outdoors.

At some time during their life, everybody will measure something. This is usually in the context of a practical activity such as weighing ingredients for a cake, holding a jumper against yourself to see if it will fit, using a tape measure to find out how much curtain material you need or looking at a watch to see how long it took to walk to the bus stop. Learning how to measure and compare different sizes and different objects is an important life skill that contributes to our understanding of the concept of length, weight, capacity and time.

It is not surprising then that children learn most about measurement (including the words to describe what they have found out about the size of objects) when they are engaged in a range of hands-on activities. Children's knowledge of the vocabulary of measurement develops during everyday conversations with adults and with each other. They hear and make comments such as, "This bag is really heavy" and "How tall you've grown".

An important stage of understanding measurement takes place when children begin to understand the idea of comparison as a measuring technique. Children's

fascination with the size of things often starts from stories, e.g. big giants, small beetles, the Three Billy Goats Gruff or the Three Bears who all have equipment such as bowls, beds and chairs proportionate to their size. The biggest bear has the biggest bed, the smallest bear the smallest bed and so on – of course this is often reflected in children's real lives, as they most probably sleep in smaller beds and use smaller plates, cups and cutlery than the adults they know. Their understanding develops as they directly compare the big spoons and their small spoons during mealtimes and when they play with large beach balls and small throwing balls. This is especially so when adults draw attention to and compare the sizes of different objects.

Children do, however, need some support and a lot of relevant experiences to develop an understanding of conservation of measures, i.e. the idea that the length of a piece of ribbon is still the same when it is rolled up, that a ball of dough still weighs the same when it is rolled out. Perhaps the hardest concept of all for children to come to terms with is that the juice in the small wide jug is still the same amount when poured into the tall thin container.

Children learn about measurement by measuring lots of things and they need lots of interactive experiences to hone their expertise. Not only do they need a wealth of opportunities to measure, they also need lots of practice at using measuring equipment such as weighing scales and tape measures, as well as jugs and counting spoonfuls, so that they can become competent measurers.

Young children learn to use a range of measuring words such as heavy, light, full and empty by being involved in and discussing hands-on activities. The aim is to hear all our children questioning, debating and talking about measuring things.

Through dramatic play, children often discover and use mathematical concepts such as measurement, providing they have access to enough resources that enable them to weigh, make lists, count money, measure heights, write numbers on labels, etc. Through play, they can develop the measuring skills that are a regular part of everyday life. Support the children by ensuring measuring equipment is close at hand and that you engineer discussions on measurement – this will enable both you and the children to use the appropriate vocabulary. Where you can, infiltrate measuring equipment into an area. For instance, you could put out measuring spoons on a sensory table and measuring rulers in the graphics area.

Whenever possible involve the children in the preparation and choice of materials for an activity.

Reading, writing, making and collecting recipes are enjoyable ways into using measures. Children can invent their own recipes for making cakes, perfume or vegetable mash. They could invent a range of sandwiches with different fillings and vote for their favourite. You can also use biscuit cutters to cut the sandwiches into different sizes and shapes. Any recipe can be made into a zigzag picture book of instructions so that other children can make it. Read together *The Giant Jam Sandwich* by Vernon Lord and Janet Burroway (Boardbooks, 2009). Try a cake recipe where all the ingredients are weighed against an egg or make speculative remarks such as 'I wonder how many raisins you can get in an egg cup?'

Use everyday routines and events such as snack time or story time as an opportunity to talk about the size of objects: 'this looks like a very large book'; 'here is quite a small apple'. These situations can aid language development as well as thinking and talking maths, but remember that the starting point will always be the child, their interests and their curiosity about the world and its resources.

Exciting snakes stimulate talk about length.

Length

Length is usually the first measurement that children become familiar with, and can work with and understand. Measuring and estimating length is easier than other measures as it is a very visual measure and it is often easy to make direct comparisons. Children can compare the height of two teddies by standing them next to each other. Comparing horizontal lengths (e.g. laying two sticks on the ground or pencils on the table) is more difficult as children need to be aware that the objects they are comparing should start at the same point, level with each other. You will need to draw children's attention to this.

Initiate experiences that develop children's understanding of the language of comparison in length. Be sensitive about comparing children's height, foot or head size with each other, and instead introduce the vocabulary of comparison such as longer than, wider than, taller than, high, higher, highest using teddies, dolls, toys, constructions, pencils, ribbons and sticks.

Most young children work with informal units when they first start to measure length. These units can be body measures such as footsteps, strides or handspans, or they may choose to use felt tip pen lengths, blocks, beans or pennies. Later they can count strides along chalk lines to check which line is the longest or use bricks to measure the height of a sunflower.

One of the key concepts of measurement is conservation: in terms of length this is the idea that a piece of string will still be the same length if you arrange it from a straight line into a circle or wavy line. Children will of course be much older before they understand transitivity – the ability to accurately measure a length using a standard measure and to then draw another line of the same length. You can help children towards developing these skills and concepts when you are talking about length by using hand movements to describe size. For example, hold your hands far apart when you are describing how long the worm was, or indicate with your hands and eyes how tall the giant was – this will give children a visual clue.

Make sure the resources provided include a selection of ribbons, paper strips, string and sticks for quick measurement activities. Provide linking elephants or cubes for non-standard measuring as well as large counters, Cuisenaire rods and Numicon plates. You should also include a height chart, surveyor's tape, trundle wheels and metre sticks, tape measures and number lines as well as small rulers.

Essential length vocabulary

Long, longer than, longest, as long as	Thick
	Thin
Short, shorter than, shortest	Deep
Tall, taller than, tallest	Shallow
High, higher than	The same length as, the same height as
Low	Measure
Wide	Compare
Narrow	

Five steps in understanding length

Step 1.
Child describes all length or height measurements as big or small, and refers to places as being 'a long way away' regardless of the length of the journey.

Step 2.
Child describes sizes and can compare when related to self, e.g. 'my brother is littler than me'; 'the boots are too small'.

Step 3.
Child uses an increasing number of words to describe lengths and measures lengths during play.

Step 4.
Child uses non-standard length measuring equipment with accuracy and can compare one length with another.

Step 5.
Child is beginning to relate distance and time taken to travel there.

Length – experiences and activities

Make a length

Take the opportunity during children's play to line up cars, dinosaurs, plastic bears and any other small world characters. When the children become interested in the lines you are making, collect together an assortment of small objects such as buttons, counters, corks, paper clips and anything else that will remain stationary and not roll. Lay down two pieces of ribbon a short distance apart and suggest the children fill the space between the two ribbons with some of the objects from the collection. When children are successful at this activity challenge them to make a longer or shorter line. Discuss such issues as where they started the line of objects and where the line finished.

Line them up

You need:

- a 1–3 dice

- a collection of small bricks.

Play a dice game where the object of the game is to build a line of bricks across the table. Take it in turns to toss a 1–3 dice and put that many bricks in the line. The person to add the last brick to the line when it reaches the other side of the table could be the winner. Talk about whether the line went straight across the table and describe how the bricks go from one edge of the table to the other. You can play this game outside by drawing two chalk lines on the ground and using any outdoor equipment to make the line of objects from chalk line to chalk line.

String

Resource the craft table with pieces of string, all the same length. Provide children with two pieces of string and together compare them; talk about the fact that the strings are the same length. Encourage the children to arrange each piece of string into a different shape and finally to glue the string onto a piece of paper. Support them in writing a display label to explain that all the strings are the same length. You can extend this activity into the outdoor area by laying some lengths of skipping rope or string on the floor in different shapes. Ask children to walk along the rope and guess which piece of rope is the longest/shortest.

Dough worms

Dough can be rolled, stretched and measured. When children are working with dough encourage them to make worms and then to decide who has made the longest and the shortest worm. Choose a short worm and talk about rolling the dough to make a worm longer than that one. Join the worms together to see if they can stretch the whole length of the table. Make comments about the different lengths of worm and encourage the children to say how they know which worm is the longest or shortest.

Outdoor trails

In the outdoor area provide a box of small twigs and sticks – show the children how to make arrows by laying three sticks on the ground. Together, use the sticks to make a trail to follow; discuss how far apart the arrows need to be and whether the trail is a long or short one. Don't forget the trail will need to lead somewhere e.g. to the sandpit or to a secret den made by throwing a curtain over a washing line. Alternatively, the children could discover a large dinosaur or a small teddy at the end of the trail. Encourage the children to make their own trails. An adaptation of the activity could be to ask children to draw chalk arrows on the tarmac or to use cut-out paper footprints. (For more ideas on maths trails see page 83)

Paint a length

Help the children to tape different lengths and widths of paper to the ground in the outdoor area. Resource the area with different sizes of paint roller, trays and a range of coloured paints; invite the children to use a roller to apply 'a length' of paint to one of the pieces of paper. As they make different sized lengths with the paint rollers take the opportunity to introduce the relevant length vocabulary. Discuss whether the yellow length is longer than the green or whether it is the same size. When the activity is finished arrange the painted lengths in order of size.

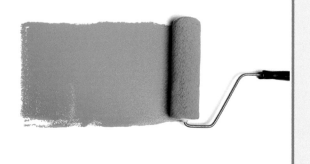

Growing tall

Keep a record of fast-growing plants such as sunflowers, amaryllis, cress and carrot tops or cut and come lettuce (lettuce which continues to grow when leaves are removed). The measurements can take the form of comparison if the children use some coloured sticks of various lengths. Discussions can then focus on, for example, whether or not the amaryllis has grown taller than the red stick.

Make a measuring tape

Encourage children who are interested in measuring different lengths to draw round one of their hands, cut it out and use it as a template to produce more hands. This is fairly easy to do if you use the template on folded newsprint paper as the children can cut out several hands at once. When the child has a set of about ten hands, use sticky tape to make a line of hands and then roll this up to use as a measuring tape. Support the child in measuring lengths that are longer or shorter than their ten hand-span tape. Encourage the children to make a collection of objects that are about the same length as their ten hand-span tape.

Weight

Children need considerable experience of handling, weighing and comparing different objects to develop an understanding of the key ideas relating to weight. Weighing activities can be a lot of fun for young children especially if they involve filling containers with different materials and weighing them. The activities also provide you with an opportunity to introduce words such as lighter and heavier as the children play. While children develop their ideas about weight, the most beneficial experiences they can have are play situations involving the need to use words that describe and compare weight, e.g. heavy and heavier than. They also need support from adults who can introduce and extend their use of the vocabulary of weight.

An important concept, regarding weight, for children to establish is that the size of an object doesn't always have an effect on its weight. Understanding that heavier does not always mean bigger and smaller is not necessarily lighter is a vital step in becoming weight knowledgeable. Children develop this idea that weight is not necessarily related to size by handling lots of objects during imaginative and creative play. Similarly, they develop essential weighing skills by having opportunities to access a range of different weighing and balancing equipment.

Try and infiltrate a weighing component or reason to weigh in role play or pretend play situations. Play alongside children and model using the language of weight by giving a running commentary on any weighing experiences that are taking place. Make sure that your home corner is resourced with a variety of objects of different weights and sizes and that you regularly comment or draw children's attention to them. Check that

there are balances so that children can play at weighing cake ingredients or vegetables for soup.

Check that the shop has some scales to weigh potatoes, the builders' yard in the outdoor area has bucket balances to weigh bricks, the post office has scales to weigh parcels and the baby clinic or vet has balances to weigh baby dolls and pet toys. In dramatic play you could mime carrying a heavy parcel or shopping bag, or pretend to be a feather or leaf being blown about by the wind. In the malleable area, set up a tray containing plenty of cotton wool balls and different sized tongs. This will give children opportunities to pick up light objects and will also develop their small motor skills. Set up a block and tackle pulley system in the outdoor area to give children experience of moving very heavy weights.

Initially encourage the children to compare the weight of two objects by directly holding them in their hands. Use a couple of shopping bags – one in each hand to compare the weight of a bag of dry sand with a bag of cornflakes and decide which is the lightest. Look for situations where you can refine children's use of the language of weight. You could use as a starting point for a discussion, questions such as, 'Can you think of something in the room that you would find too heavy to lift?'

Spend time helping children to understand how a balance works. Discuss what it means if one side goes up when the objects are put in the balance buckets. Make sure the children know that if a pan goes down it contains the heavier object and conversely (what children find more difficult to appreciate) if the pan goes up the object is lighter.

Essential weight vocabulary

Lifting	Heavy, heavier than, heaviest, as heavy as
Carrying	
	About the same weight
Weighing	
Balance	Compare
Light, lighter than, lightest	

Hands-on cooking and baking activities encourage discussions about weighing and balancing.

Weight — experiences and activities

Weight walk

You need:

- a selection of soft toys
- three or four paper carrier bags.

Encourage the children to choose two soft toys from the collection, to put one each in a carrier bag and to then go for a walk round the room carrying the bags one in each hand. At the end of the walk the children say which toy is the heaviest and which toy the lightest. Try this with several different toys until they find the heaviest toy of all. Younger children will probably choose randomly which toys they put in the bags and will concentrate on finding the heaviest toy. When working with more experienced measurers and weighers you can discuss with them a more methodical way of testing to find the heaviest and then the lightest toy.

Weigh in

You need:

- a bucket balance
- some small smooth pebbles (as sold at garden centres)
- a collection of six objects to be weighed.

Suggest the children choose an object and weigh it in the bucket using the pebbles to balance it. Discuss with them how they will know when their object balances. To extend the activity provide post-it notes for the children to record how many pebbles they used to balance their object. Some children may record by drawing the number of pebbles in the bucket and others may use numerals. Together, create a chart of those recordings; draw children's attention to the different numbers that are recorded and assess whether any children can comment on which object was the heaviest by looking at the chart.

Balancing eggs and making cakes

You need:

- balance scales
- bun tins
- plastic knives

Ingredients:

- 2 large eggs
- caster sugar
- self-raising flour
- butter or margarine
- jam

(This recipe uses the same weight of eggs, flour, sugar and butter.)

Step 1: Put the two eggs on one side of the scales and take it in turns to balance the same amount of flour, butter and sugar. Draw children's attention to the balancing of each ingredient.

Step 2: Cream together the butter and sugar, add the eggs and then sieve in the flour. Alternatively, mix all the ingredients together in a food processor. If the mixture seems too dry add some teaspoonfuls of warm water.

Step 3: Grease the bun tins and put a large spoonful of the mixture in each space.

Step 4: Use the knives to make a split in the top of each cake and insert some jam.

Step 5: Cook the cakes at 170°C /gas mark 3 for 15 minutes. Wait for the cakes to cool before removing from the tins and eating.

Parcel-post play

This could be part of a post office or birthday theme or an independent activity. Set up an area with a selection of weighing equipment such as bucket balances, digital scales, spring balances, kitchen scales and bathroom scales. Talk about how different weighing machines work. Provide a selection of ready-made parcels of different weights and sizes and some ink pads and stamps. Explain that the parcels need to be weighed and stamped before delivery. Join in the play, showing how to use one of the weighing scales and stamping PAID on the parcel. Extend the activity by helping children to wrap up and weigh their own parcels.

Find it heavy

You need:

- a display table
- a bucket balance
- a dainty shoe
- a heavy book.

Set up an interactive display for children to contribute to. Talk about how to estimate weight by holding something in your hand and deciding whether it feels heavy or light. Discuss how bucket balances work and what it means when one bucket goes down low. Let the children handle the shoe and the book and decide which is heavier. Put the shoe in one side of the bucket balance and the book in the other. Together look at the balance and discuss whether the shoe or the book is heavier. Remove the book and put on the table, then challenge children to find other objects that are heavier than the shoe. When they have found and weighed the objects the children can add them to the display. Write a label explaining that these things are all heavier than the shoe and invite other contributions.

Vegetable stall

You need:

- a table
- a selection of real vegetables if possible
- weighing scales
- a till
- shopping baskets
- notices and labels including the names of the vegetables and prices.

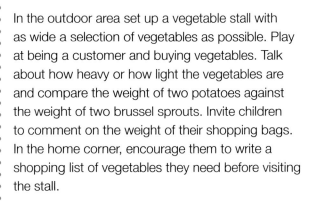

In the outdoor area set up a vegetable stall with as wide a selection of vegetables as possible. Play at being a customer and buying vegetables. Talk about how heavy or how light the vegetables are and compare the weight of two potatoes against the weight of two brussel sprouts. Invite children to comment on the weight of their shopping bags. In the home corner, encourage them to write a shopping list of vegetables they need before visiting the stall.

Extend the activity by setting up other stalls as part of a market scenario. Stalls selling fruit, bread, pretend sweets and biscuits would also provide weighing experience while others such as flower and material stalls would give valuable experience of counting and measuring length.

Vote for heavy

In this activity children pass round two identical-looking parcels and decide after handling them which is heavier. Fill two identical boxes with different dry products such as rice and cornflakes. Wrap the boxes in identical wrapping paper, then ask the children to hold both parcels and decide which is heavier. Give each child a small dinosaur and ask them to place it next to the parcel they think is heavier. When everyone has voted for the heavier parcel, weigh the parcels, say which is heavier and count the dinosaur votes. Extend the activity on another occasion by voting for the lighter parcel.

Capacity

Capacity is the amount of space inside a hollow container, and what we usually measure is how much a hollow container will hold. Capacity and weight are linked and this can be seen, for instance, in measuring jugs where 20 fluid ounces are marked as well as 1 pint. A fluid ounce is the capacity, the space in the jug, needed to contain an ounce weight of water.

Volume is the amount of space taken up by a solid shape and is measured in cubic units such as cubic centimetres. Children experience volume every time they get in the bath and see it when they slide pebbles into a bowl of water and watch the water level rise.

As adults we use mainly standard measurements such as litres or pints and gallons to talk about a container's capacity. When we are measuring volume we usually refer to cubic centimetres. Children need time to explore capacity and volume, and opportunities to fill and empty a range of different sized and shaped containers.

Capacity is a difficult concept for children to grasp. Shape and size influence their decision as to which containers will hold the most. Many young children think that if a container is taller then it must hold more, without considering other attributes. It is even more challenging for children to understand that two containers can be different shapes and heights and still hold a similar amount of juice.

It is during play that children experiment with and use various containers to grow an awareness of volume and capacity. Children develop the ideas linked to capacity measurements by talking about them, estimating, learning the vocabulary, using the tools of measuring and occasionally recording the results. Although measuring occurs naturally during the day the kind of measuring that children engage with is usually direct comparison, e.g. 'my bucket is bigger than yours'; 'you've got more juice than me'.

Children's experiences linked to capacity come from role play such as teddy bear tea parties using teapots and mugs, using buckets in the sand, using the hose outdoors to fill watering cans or filling lots of yoghurt pots with water and then pouring the water from them one at a time to fill up a basin. Put into words what the children are doing and describe their actions using the language of capacity, e.g. full, empty, overflowing, level.

Collect a range of spoons, scoops and ladles that are used for a variety of purposes to carry or measure liquids or dry ingredients. Remember to engage with the measuring equipment and materials yourself and share the experience with the children. Use sets of nesting containers to introduce a discussion about capacity. Support children in exploring and alternating between stacking the containers and fitting them one inside another, drawing their attention to why the containers fit inside each other.

Compare how many scoops of sand it takes to fill a small cup and then fill it again using spoonfuls. Demonstrate measuring skills by smoothing a level spoonful or considering whether the cup will overflow if you add more sand. Try using a small bucket to fill a large bucket, and make and use funnels to support this activity. Developing the skills of filling and emptying all aid the children's ability to compare two capacities directly (e.g. to be able to say that one jug holds more juice than another).

Give children different experiences of capacity by using a continuous pourable media such as water, dry sand or lentils as well as measuring by using discrete countable materials such as beads, bricks and pebbles.

Essential capacity vocabulary

Full	Small amount
Empty	Large amount
Nearly full	Count
Pour	Holds more
Funnel	Holds less
Container	

Capacity — experiences and activities

Making sand mousse

You need:

- dry sand
- water
- washing-up liquid
- a rotary whisk.

Make sand mousse together by whisking together in a large bowl: two cupfuls of dry sand, water and washing-up liquid. Entice children into discussion by providing teaspoons to fill very small containers with the mousse. Talk about how many containers they filled, whether it took one, two or three spoonfuls and how they knew when a container was full up.

What was in the container?

Make a collection of recycled containers, such as small cereal packets, ketchup bottles, chocolate boxes and cheese packets. Discuss with the children what they think was in each container and encourage them to explain how they knew what was originally inside. Provide the children with an extra-large packet of rice, funnels, small scoops and spoons to experiment with filling and emptying the containers. Extend the activity by challenging children to find out which container will hold the most rice.

The full and empty centre

Extend children's experience of capacity by setting up a filling and emptying centre. Put out three shallow plastic trays on a table and fill with a variety of dried beans. Provide small containers, jugs, funnels and spoons for the children to fill and empty. Regularly change the content of the trays – red lentils or rice are very satisfying to run fingers through and pour like liquid. In order that children have opportunities to compare and order capacities make sure the containers are interesting to fill and empty. Over time, prompt discussions about which containers hold the most or the least.

Filling and emptying lots of different containers is the best way to explore capacity.

Inside the box

In the outdoor area provide a large cardboard 'white goods' box such as from a washing machine. Discuss with the children how many of them they think could sit inside the large box. Test out the estimates by getting children to sit in the box and then counting. Discuss whether you could get more or fewer children in the box if they stood up. Write a notice describing how many children can fit in the box.

Pass the dolly game

Give a small group of children a set of Russian nesting dolls (or a collection of nesting boxes). Play music, and when it stops the player holding the doll unscrews the outer doll, keeps it and passes the rest of the set to the child sitting next to them. Keep playing until a player is holding the last doll (the smallest one), then together reassemble the set into one large doll.

Looking for nesting boxes

You need:

- a collection of different sized and shaped boxes.

Ask children to choose a box and then to find another box that will fit inside it, then another and another. Ask 'how can we find out which box holds the most?' Experiment with measuring capacity by filling different sized containers with the same material such as polystyrene pieces or large wooden beads.

Teeny tiny celebration cakes

This simple recipe uses capacity measures for the cake ingredients instead of weighing them. The recipe makes six small cakes baked in small 200g baked bean tins. When the children are measuring the ingredients show them how to smooth the top of the cup or spoon to make it level.

Ask each child who will be making a cake to bring in an empty 200g small baked bean tin.

You need:

- a small bow
- a large mixing bowl
- a jug
- a wooden spoon
- a fork
- six 200g baked bean tins

Ingredients:

- 1 cup of mixed dried fruit
- 1 cup self-raising flour
- 1 cup soft brown sugar
- 1 half teaspoon of each of the following: mixed spice, cinnamon, ground nutmeg
- 1 large beaten egg
- 65g melted butter
- 1 tablespoon orange juice
- 1 tablespoon apricot jam
- 2 tablespoons milk

Step 1: In a small bowl, pour the orange juice over the dried fruit, stir and leave aside.

Step 2: Grease the baked bean tins. Into the mixing bowl sift the flour, spice, cinnamon and nutmeg and stir in the brown sugar.

Step 3: In a jug mix together the milk, the beaten egg, apricot jam and melted butter. Pour into the mixing bowl and stir, then pour in the dried fruit mixture and stir gently until all the ingredients are mixed into a thick lumpy batter.

Step 4: Divide the mixture between the six greased baked bean tins. Bake for 20 minutes at 200°C/gas mark 6. Leave in the tins for 10 minutes, remove cakes and cool on a wire rack.

Step 5: When the cakes are cold children can cut circles of ready-made icing to cover the top of each cake, decorate the icing and tie a ribbon round each cake.

Time

Most children find the concept of time difficult and a true understanding of time can take some years to develop because of its abstract nature. Children are usually of primary school age before they understand and can calculate time. Some young children learn the skill of reading the clock face (especially the hourly o'clock times) but without a true understanding of time.

Comprehension of time has two aspects: first the skill of reading a clock face and saying the time with a link to calculating time differences, and second the ability to sequence events (as in a story or happenings during the day) and use the vocabulary of time. This sequencing and related language is the emphasis in the early years.

For many children time only exists in the present, in the here and now, and they may find it more difficult to remember past events than to imagine a coming birthday, for example. Keeping a group or class diary as a focus for discussion offers opportunities to talk about what happened yesterday and what might happen tomorrow. Personalize the diary by inviting comments on what occurs during the day. Focus on referring to a class birthday chart at least weekly, identifying whose birthday is next and reflecting on past birthdays.

Make sure that the children have access to a range of timers and set them challenges such as 'I wonder how many hops you can do in 10 seconds or before the sand runs out?' Although young children are unlikely to be able to tell the time using an analogue clock you can involve them in observing the clock face by asking them to remind you about an event such as snack time e.g. when the clock shows ten o'clock. Alert children to the passage of time by making observations such as 'Well we tidied away the bricks in five minutes – that must be a record'.

Remembering the sequence of calendar time such as days of the week or the names of the months in order is out of the grasp of most young children. Instead, help children to sequence the events of their day, e.g. the common reoccurring activities such as wake up, have breakfast and so on. Make sure that children have ample opportunity to talk about routines and sequences of events that are part of their lives. A starting point might be what they did at the weekend, children's own news or to reflect on or anticipate the key events during the week using the words yesterday, today and tomorrow. When describing or reflecting on an event together, say when it happened: 'Do you remember it was before we went to the park?'; 'I thought you built the castle after we had snack time'. This provides the children with something to use as a marker in time. Draw attention to distances and make connections with other measurements.

As you begin to tell a story you could emphasize the opening phrases 'once upon a time' or 'a long time ago'. When you have finished reading a story, discuss with the group the sequence of events. Use a hand puppet to retell the story in the children's own words using prompts such as 'What happened first?' Describe incidents in the story with the puppet professing not to know, for example, when the dragon arrived and asking the group for help. The children will be very keen to help the puppet remember the sequence of events in the story.

Essential time vocabulary

Before	Minute	Today, tomorrow, yesterday
After	Days of the week	
Soon	Faster	Early, earlier
Next	Slower	Late, later
Long ago	About the same time	Birthday
Day		Month
Night	Quicker	
Hour	Stop	

Time — experiences and activities

Night and day game

Discuss with the children the differences between night and day, and how they know whether it is day or night-time. Talk about the routines that occur during the day and encourage the children to role play some of these. Make comments such as 'If you're pretending to eat porridge it must be daytime'; 'If you're putting on pyjamas it must be night-time'. When the children have rehearsed a few actions play the 'Night and day game'. Show a large circle on a stick with the sun on one side and the moon on the other. Explain that you are going to play some music; when it stops they should look and see whether the sun or the moon is showing and act out something that happens at this time. Extend the activity by showing the children how to make their own night and day circles.

O'clock number line

You need:

* twelve paper circles each numbered as a clock face

* a washing line

* twelve pegs.

Use 12 paper circles to make a number line of clock faces. Draw in the hands with each clock face showing a different hour time. Help the children to peg each clock face on a washing line in the correct sequence. Support the children in saying one o'clock, two o'clock, three o'clock and so on. Remove a clock face and ask the children to suggest what the missing clock time is.

When I was a baby

Ask children to bring in a photograph of themselves as a baby. Make a display of the photos and discuss the differences between themselves as babies and now. Together make a list of what they can do now, including things such as run, jump, say their own name. Take contributions from everyone and attach the comment to each photograph. Use words/phrases such as then, now and long time ago.

How fast?

Explore time by observing how long a container takes to empty of water, comparing this with other containers. Resource the water tray with a range of different sized funnels and small jugs. Provide a collection of empty litre water bottles with a series of holes pierced in the sides. Ask questions such as 'which bottle do you think will empty first and which last?'; 'how could we make the water run out faster?'

Lets talk about birthdays

Show the children a birthday card with an age number on it. Initiate a discussion around how old children are and the ages of other children they might know. Ask questions such as 'is that older or younger than you?' Together make three large birthday cards that have the headings 'We are 3', 'We are 4' and 'We are 5' (or cards relevant to the ages of the children you are working with). Take an individual photograph of each child and encourage them to stick it in the appropriate card. Remind them to change cards as their birthday occurs. Extend the activity by making a monthly class birthday chart for the children to refer to.

Beat the clock

You need:

- a bowl of small objects
- a paper plate
- tongs
- a 1 minute sand or oven timer.

Children count how many objects they can take out of the bowl and can put on the plate using the tongs, before the timer runs out. Encourage them to have several turns and decide which was their fastest. Extend the activity by using the timer to time other things such as how many jumps or hops or beads they can thread.

Clock repairs-r-us

Set up a clock-repair table where children can investigate and take apart redundant clocks and watches. Discuss any numbers that might be on a clock face and explore setting the alarm on kitchen timers. Extend the activity by including other timing devices such as sand timers and stop watches.

Tocker races

You need:

- a selection of circular lids from coffee jars or similar shaped containers to make the 'tockers'
- circles of paper the same size as the lids
- small pieces of Plasticine.

Challenge the children to make a long rocking 'tocker'. Ask them to draw a design or picture on the paper circle and then fit it inside the lid. Stand the lid up on its edge and put a small piece of Plasticine inside the rim of the lid to act as a balance. Show the children how to make the lid rock backwards and forwards and talk about which lids tock longest.

Trips in the local environment help children to think about time — how long did we wait for the bus?

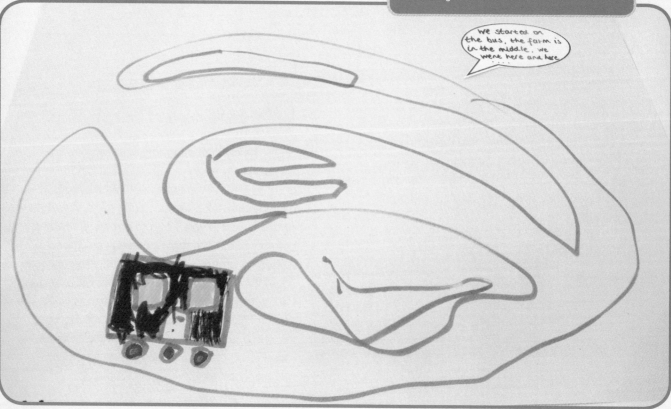

An opportunity for mixing, talking and finding out more about measures.

The role of the adult

Understanding measurement comes firstly from talking about measures and using the vocabulary of measuring in statements and questions, and secondly from comparing different objects, e.g. by holding two potatoes and deciding which is heavier, or putting two pencils next to each other and deciding which is longer.

The following experiences and activities help children understand about measurement:

- **rehearsing the language of measuring in practical situations**

- **playing at measuring in lots of different areas**

- **working in a range of media where length and weight measurement is important**

- **experiencing both wet and dry sand when using different sized containers**

- **estimating how many steps or strides to reach the climbing frame**

- **identifying the heaviest or lightest object among objects they are sorting**

- **comparing strings of beads to find out which is the longest**

- **using a calendar or a diary to find out what is happening that day**

- **keeping a measuring journal to document what they have measured each week.**

Enriching provision

Children need to experiment with measuring in lots of different situations in order to have opportunities to use a variety of measuring words. Take advantage of the everyday situations in which measuring can arise, such as working with play dough, building a castle, making bead snakes, using water squirts, constructing a wheeled transport route, or filling a basket or box.

In the book area, tell stories and read books that have an element of measurement. There are a lot of traditional stories with a focus on the language of size comparison such as *The Three Bears, The Three Billy Goats Gruff* and *The Enormous Turnip*. Of course, stories and rhymes are very much a part of supporting children in becoming competent at comparing sizes. Look at stories that focus on giants, decide together whether the giant would be able to sit on one of their chairs without it breaking or how much space the giant would need, and include children's own experiences of measuring.

In the outdoor area create an environment such as a shop or market stall that encourages conversation about the size and weight of various fruits and vegetables. Organize an outdoor scavenger hunt where the children look for objects of a certain length.

In the construction area model the appropriate language and involve children in discussion about measuring situations, e.g. 'You are right – I think the road that you built is longer than mine'; 'I wonder how many bricks it takes to build a bigger castle?'; 'Has anyone an idea how we could measure how much sand this bucket holds?' Together, collect and sort all the long building bricks or estimate whether a bridge is wide enough for a toy lorry to go through.

In the role-play area, provide resources that encourage children to use their measuring skills. Look for situations and contexts that give children the opportunity to compare objects by length, height, weight and capacity.

For more experienced measurers, help children to take photographs of local buildings, trees and lamp posts. Pin up a washing line vertically against a wall so that children can compare the item in each photograph and then assemble them into a height line. Involve the children in producing ideas for signs and posters about measurements in your setting.

Open-ended questions and enabling statements about measurement

I wonder if anything is longer than the red ribbon?

I'm not sure which bag is heavier.

What can you say about the weight of this bear?

How long does it take to make?

I think I'll measure that again to make sure.

I wonder if we've collected enough conkers to fill this box?

Can you tell everybody how you know that the blue box holds the most?

Maths home challenges

Filling and emptying

Collect together some small empty containers and some yoghurt pots (or egg cups).

Fill up one of the containers with water and then use the yoghurt pots to empty it.

Now use the yoghurt pot to fill the container up with water.

Can you find in your home two containers that hold the same amount of water?

And

Can you find two containers that hold a different amount of water?

Can you draw the containers?

Have fun!

Measuring height

The tallest animals in the world are giraffes which are 3.5 metres (17 feet) tall.

Measure the tallest person who lives in your house. See how many different ways you can find to measure their height:

- You could try using a piece of ribbon or string

or

- You could ask them to lie on the floor and see how many forks and spoons long they are.

Then you could ask someone to measure how long you are in forks and spoons.

Have fun!

Where is Teddy?

Hide your favourite teddy and then ask an adult to see if they can find it. Tell them when they are getting close to the teddy by saying 'hot' and when they are getting further away from the teddy by saying 'cold'.

When they have found the teddy ask them to hide him so that you can look for him.

Have fun!

© Foundations of Mathematics (Featherstone, an imprint of Bloomsbury Publishing plc)

Solving problems

Challenging children to solve their own maths problems.

Active problem solving occurs when we give young children the opportunity to choose, reason and make decisions. Challenging them to solve mathematical problems, talking about their observations, as well as estimating and predicting all help and inspire children to enjoy mathematical learning. These strategies also support children in persevering if the problem solving becomes difficult. When children are involved in solving problems on a regular basis it challenges them to make sense of their knowledge and experiences, and of the maths they know. It is incredibly exciting and empowering for children when they are involved in daily problem-solving situations, especially sharing ideas with others, coming up with solutions and then reflecting together on their mathematical successes.

The problems children are solving should always make sense to them and have relevance to the world they are operating in. They should focus mainly on hands-on, play-based activities or develop from play-based experiences.

Problem solving in young children involves them understanding and using two kinds of maths:

- **Maths knowledge – that is, learning and applying some aspect of maths such as counting, calculating or measuring.**

- **Maths thinking skills – that is, reasoning, predicting, talking the problem through, making connections, generalizing, identifying patterns and finding solutions.**

The play-based problem-solving challenges children are involved in should aim to support them in using the maths they know to reach a solution. You can support their thinking processes by volunteering ideas, such as asking if they have a plan, or by encouraging them to think how they can collect and organize the information or data they have found. Children will be more successful problem solvers if they have access to multi-sensory materials to support their thinking.

When children are solving problems they must use the maths knowledge that is appropriate to the situation. They will need to identify, for example, that this is an 'adding situation' or 'we need to count' to find a solution. Similarly, with maths thinking skills children will need to use the appropriate skill for that particular problem, e.g. identifying when they need to look for a pattern or predict a result before finding a solution. Therefore, in order for children to have the opportunity to use a range of thinking skills and maths knowledge, adults must try to see the maths problem-solving potential in everyday activities.

For a problem to be successfully solved, children first need to identify what the problem is and then decide what maths they need to do to help them find the solution. Finally, they need to realize that yes, they have solved the problem. A crucial time for learning is when children are discussing with you their proposed solutions and offering their ideas on what might happen. It is then that opportunities for creativity in their maths thinking occur. You can support this by giving a few encouraging nods, smiles and murmurs and resisting the urge to suggest your own solution. Let children do as much of their own solution finding as they possibly can.

Choice is a vital part of problem solving. For instance, when young learners are sorting it is important they make the decision about how to sort the objects they

Maths problems often arise from thought-provoking imaginative small-world play scenarios.

have collected together, rather than an adult suggesting a particular way of sorting things out. When the problem they have set themselves, albeit not verbalized, of how to sort out their collection is solved, invite the children to make statements about what they have collected and the decisions they made along the way.

A key element of mathematical problem solving for young learners is that it involves choices and opportunities to reason and make decisions, and uses and builds on the maths knowledge they are already secure in. To support children when they are problem solving, consolidate their maths knowledge and thinking skills by discussing possibilities with them. Talking about what they are doing as well as asking low-key questions while they are problem solving helps children organize their ideas and later explain what they have done. This should enable you to make the following observational assessments of children as they are working, playing and problem solving:

- **showing an interest in number problems and using their own methods to find solutions**

- **organizing and sorting objects and being able to explain what they are doing**

- **choosing the materials and equipment that they want to work with and offering solutions to problems**

- **beginning to justify the decisions they have made**

- **using number, counting and calculation to solve problems**

- **using a variety of shapes to make patterns, pictures, models and constructions and explaining how they made them.**

Whatever the aspect of maths children are learning and whatever the problem they are trying to solve, the quality of engagement with them is of central importance. Adopt a 'softly, softly' approach: wonder a lot rather than using too many direct questions. An important role for adults when children are problem solving is to model any new vocabulary and support children as they practise using this (especially calculation words) to say aloud how they solved the problem. This will be easier for children if they have already heard you commenting on and summarizing what they were doing. Recap what the problem is that they are solving and retell how the problem was solved.

Six key questions and enabling statements that support problem solving

> I wonder what will happen if you add another one?

> Can you remember what we were trying to find out?

> What do you think you will need?

> What can we say about...?

> Can you explain...?

> Can anyone think of another idea?

Using mathematical graphics to make sense of and support mathematical thinking.

Essential problem-solving vocabulary

Number	Compare
Too many	Similar
Too few	Same
Enough	Find out
Not enough	Look at
Talk about	Remember
Explain	Imagine
Show us	Listen
Check	Decide
Sort	Vote
Match	Solution

Solving problems— experiences and activities

Building dens

Building dens outdoors is a good way to involve children in some measuring and mathematical problem solving, especially if they are part of the construction team. Make sure that the children themselves identify the resources they need. Encourage them to think about the position and size of the den and how many children should be able to sit inside it. Support the acitivty by offering advice on joining materials with things such as bulldog clips or duct tape. Take photographs during the construction to support children's reflective account of how the den was built. Extend the activity by displaying the photographs using labels such as 'first we . . .'; 'second we looked for . . .'

Story maths

The problem-solving scenario in this activity focuses on calculating and list-making. Use a puppet and artefacts to tell a story and explain to the children that the puppet sometimes makes mistakes. They should listen out for any he might make so they can help him understand more maths. The first story the puppet tells could be about going shopping and using pennies to buy different items for lunch. Extend the activity by suggesting that children help the puppet by making a shopping list so that he doesn't forget to buy things.

Weaving boxes

You need:

- shoe boxes with large elastic bands or circles of narrow elastic stretched between the two longer sides

- lengths of different types of yarns, such as an assortment of different coloured and textured knitting wools, narrow ribbon, coloured strings and parcel ribbons.

The problem-solving aspect of this activity focuses on making choices and identifying patterns. Collect together some materials made from thick threads – talk with the children about the patterns that are made and how the threads are interwoven. Help them examine the materials with magnifying glasses and use words such as under and over. Show children the shoe boxes and encourage them to create patterns by choosing a thread and weaving it over and under the elastic bands from short side to short side. Talk together about their choices of thread and how they made their patterns. Extend the activity by displaying the shoe box patterns and inviting comments.

Take away bears game

This is a game for two children to play together, involving decision-making and strategy. Put ten bears in a line. When it is their turn the child can take one or two bears; whoever has to take the last bear is the runner-up. Play the game lots of times and discuss ideas such as whether it is best to be the player who starts and whether the strategy should always be to take one bear or two.

Guess what's missing

In this problem-solving game children use their knowledge of calculations together with the skills of predicting and justifying. Play versions of Kim's Game several times: put ten items on a tray and show the children, count them together and establish how many there are. Secretly remove two or three objects. Ask children how many you have taken away. Check by counting how many remain on the tray. Share the different ways that children have solved the problem. If it is appropriate show the children how they can find out how many have been taken by counting up on their fingers.

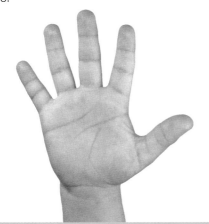

Boxing up

You need:

- a basket

- four small boxes labelled with four different numerals such as 2, 4, 5, 8

- a collection of small objects that correspond with the numerals you have chosen, for example two bears, four elephants, five counters, eight wooden beads.

In this activity children problem solve by making connections and using counting skills. Mix all the objects in a basket. Explain to the children that the objects have got muddled up and need to be sorted into the right boxes. When everything has been sorted into the smaller boxes, ask the children to explain how they did it. Look for children making the connection between, for instance, four similar objects and the box showing the numeral 4.

Bus passengers

You need:

- six small boxes to act as buses, each one labelled with a single-digit number over five

- a collection of small world characters

- a 1–6 dice.

Children playing this game are also involved in a lot of decision-making and counting. The children roll the dice and choose that number of characters. They decide in which bus to put their characters; they can either put them all in one bus or distribute them among the buses, but need to follow the rule that the number of passengers must not exceed the number on the bus. The game is over when all the buses have the correct number of passengers. Extend the activity by rolling the dice and removing passengers from the buses until they are all empty.

Domino sort

You need:

- a full box of double-six dominoes (28 dominoes).

This activity is for a small group and requires children to solve a problem by using calculation and counting skills together with organizing and finding solutions. Ask the children to choose a domino from the box and discuss with them how many spots there are on each of their chosen dominoes. Establish that a domino can have no spots, or one spot, or two spots and so on up to twelve spots. Secretly remove one domino and ask the children to discover which domino is missing from the set. Extend the problem by suggesting that they find out which particular number has the most dominoes with that total of spots.

What's in the box?

You need:

- a small box with an object inside it.

This activity gives children the opportunity to predict, estimate and justify the statements they make. Shake the box and ask the children to imagine what might be inside. Take suggestions and summarize by saying that although they might not have known for sure what was in the box they did know what was definitely not in the box. Encourage the children to say what was not in the box and to justify their suggestion. Talk about how, for instance, it couldn't be a real elephant because the box wasn't big enough; it certainly couldn't be a felt tip pen because the pen is too long; it's not cotton wool because that wouldn't make a rattling noise.

Pot lids

You need:

- some pots, boxes and tins, all with detachable lids

- a range of very different materials such as counters, beads, pennies, rice, small world characters, items that will fit in some containers and not in others.

The children involved in this problem-solving activity use their knowledge of shape and decision-making skills. Put out the collection of different containers with lids (separately). Suggest the children choose a container, identify the lid that fits it and then decide what to fill their container with. Discuss how they knew which lid to choose. Make a display of the filled containers.

Party puppet bags

You need:

- a collection of small party bags (or any other bags that have a gusset edge)

- some collage materials

- blank zigzag books.

This activity offers children opportunities to use their knowledge of shape and space as well as decision-making skills as they turn their ideas into reality. Show the children how to fit their hand in a party bag to make a puppet; suggest they decorate the bag and turn it into a character. Encourage the children to discuss what character they could make e.g. a tiger, a superhero or a princess. Support them as they identify what materials they are going to use to make their puppet. When the bags are decorated, suggest the children play puppets. Those who wish can also write or draw instructions on how to make a puppet from a party bag, in a zigzag book.

Guess the number game

You need:

- a selection of 1–10 wooden numerals or numeral cards

- a 1–10 number line

- a small pillowcase.

The problem-solving focus here relates to using number knowledge and prediction to identify a numeral. Secretly put one of the numerals in the pillowcase and ask the children to guess what the number is. Explain that they can ask questions and you will give some clues. Use words such as 'more than', 'less than' and 'between' and at the same time indicate on the number line the numbers which are more than or less than a particular number.

Problem solving on a maths trail

Following a trail or going on a maths walk is a good way of encouraging children to begin to collaborate and to work in a group to solve the problem of where to go next on the trail. Try to set aside time when children have finished a trail to reflect on the route they took and what they noticed – this will give the group the opportunity to use positional language and also to talk about the decisions they made. You could try setting up the following trails and walks in your outdoor area or nearest green space:

Colour trail

Take some material colour swatches or paint brochures and identify objects of a similar colour. Compare and make decisions such as whether the green material you are holding is the same, lighter or darker than the grass. Use drawings to record the objects that were found.

Photographic trail

The day before the trail takes place, you need to photograph and print out features in your outdoor area. Display the photographs in a line in the outdoor area and encourage the children to identify then run and touch the particular item. Extend the activity by arranging the photographs in a different order or printing the photographs into a zigzag book for groups to walk a continuous circular trail until they get back to the start.

Arrow trail

Cut out some arrow shapes from newspaper or make some arrows using twigs. Lay a trail for the children to follow around your outdoor area, making sure that the trail finishes at a particular point rather than just petering out. Children are encouraged by knowing that there is something to find at the end of the trail, e.g. a shiny bouncy ball or the three bears in a box.

Footprint line

Give the children a lot of cut-out footprints to make their own trail. You could suggest they choose two pieces of outdoor equipment to lay their route between. Encourage followers of the route to suggest where they think the route will end and why they think it will end there.

Plan stimulating maths trails to inspire and engage children.

Number trail

There are different ways for children to follow a number trail; with older children you could take a group into the local area and either look for numbers in sequence or using clipboards make a tally of how many times children see a particular number. Encourage them to predict which number they will see the most times. Younger children who are still learning to recognise different numerals will find it helpful to focus on a particular number, so laying a trail using just one number for them to follow means that they are looking for and familiarizing themselves with one outline. Cut out large photocopies of one particular number, for example five, and make a trail just using fives; in this case you could organize the five trail to end with a box containing five items.

A shape walk

This can either take place in the outdoor area searching for hidden 2D shapes or a walk in the local area identifying shapes in buildings and natural objects. As with numbers you can either focus on looking for one particular shape such as a circle or identify shapes the children notice.

A scavenger or collecting walk

This is a useful activity given that young children are much more interested in arranging materials they have collected rather than given ones. As a result their sorting at the end of the walk is of a richer dimension.

Problem solving using number

Talking is an important link between doing problem solving, solving some number problems and really understanding about number. Explaining what they are thinking helps children make sense of what they know, and this is especially important when children are solving problems. Adults are not the only potential talk partners for children; setting up experiences and activities with a focus on the children explaining to each other what they are thinking gives them responsibility for presenting images that can be recalled and revisited, and which will support any recording they may wish to do.

When children play games, they solve problems as they arise – sometimes changing the rules as they go.

Long words

Talk about the number of letters in children's names, asking questions such as 'Have you got more than five letters in your name?' and challenging them to find a shorter or longer name. Set problems by wondering aloud how the children can find out which is the longest name they know, or how many letters most children's names have. You could demonstrate using a tally to record their findings.

Number pick-up

Talk about this problem in pairs. Together sequence numerals or number cards 1 to 10 in a line and ask the children to take it in turns to pick up the numbers in order. As one of the children picks up the number five, ask who will pick up eight. Encourage them to describe how they worked it out. Extend the problem by asking 'but what would happen if three children were picking up numbers – who would pick up eight then?' Suggest that three children try it out to see if their solution was correct and again encourage them to describe how they solved the problem.

Give and take game

Play this game with a small group. The activity provides children with opportunities for talking, decision-making and calculation.

You need:

- six small objects (such as bears) for each player

- a 1–6 dice

- a line of seven objects such as toy elephants.

Make a line of seven elephants where everyone in the group can reach them and give a collection of six objects to each child. Players take it in turns to throw the dice and then make a line of objects of the same number. They may do this either by taking away some objects from the line and putting them with their collection, or adding some objects from their collection to the line. They then pass the dice to next child who throws it and repeats the process. After three rounds of the game, everyone counts their collection and decides whether they have more, fewer or the same number of objects as they started with.

Problems involving doubling, halving and sharing

Some children become very interested in certain aspects of numbers – including sharing real objects in different ways and doubling and halving quantities of real objects. In the early years, doubling, halving and sharing is only appropriate in hands-on, practical situations.

A good approach is to present the problem in a personal way – children are often more interested in 'real life' problems that affect them, their family and friends. Consider using food, picnics or parties as a starting point.

The biscuit problem

Use 12 real biscuits, or salt dough biscuits, arranged on an interesting plate. Talk to children about parties and the biscuits and count them together. Provide one plate for each child and play a game in pairs: 'Let's share the biscuits – how can we make it fair?' If the children don't suggest so, guide them towards taking turns to take a biscuit and place it on their own plate. How many biscuits each?

Put all the biscuits back on one plate. What happens if three children each have a plate, and take turns to take a biscuit? How many biscuits each? What happens with four children? What about five children – can the biscuits be shared fairly? Discuss with the children how else could you change or extend the problem, for example, by changing the number of biscuits to ten or inviting some more children to join the group. You can extend the problem solving by reading and acting out the story *The Doorbell Rang* by Pat Hutchins (Harper Trophy, 1989).

The best problems are personal – use 'mini-mes' to enhance children's small-world explorations of sharing.

Picnics

Plan a picnic with the children, selecting favourite soft toys as the picnickers. With the children, choose the food that is needed – pizza slices, crisps, cake, drinks and fruit. Ask the children how many of each item to provide for each toy. So for five toys, you may choose to have in total:

- ten slices of pizza
- fifteen biscuits or cakes
- five drinks
- ten apples and oranges

Share out the food fairly. Talk about scenarios such as what would happen if one toy didn't want to eat. Ask questions such as 'how could the food be shared out then?' and make statements such as 'I wonder what we'll do if another toy joins the picnic?' Establish by discussion and by voting if necessary whether or not the children want to add more food, more toys or take something away.

Trying it on

You need:

- a laundry basket filled with coats, hats, scarves, boots and gloves.

Ask one child to put on whatever clothes they wish. Count the items of clothing together: how many scarves, boots, hats and gloves. Make a tally of the relevant clothing. Now ask another child to copy what the first child has put on. Discuss together, make connections between the numbers and adapt the tally. Ask 'if one child has one scarf, how many do two children have?' and show using fingers how to solve the problem. Talk about two boots on one child and how many boots there would be on two children – decide together how to find a solution. When both children are wearing the same amount of clothing reflect on doubling one item and doubling two items. Based on this idea of two children wearing exactly the same, encourage the children to invent problems to ask each other, such as 'Six pieces of clothing for one child so how many items altogether?' Show the children how to prove their answer in a practical way by laying out six items of clothing and then another six items.

Play dough and bun trays

Provide the children with play dough, cutters, rolling pins, cake cases and bun tins with 6 and 12 holes. Support them as they explore ways of sharing the cakes and biscuits they make out of playdough between the bun trays. Focus on what problems they identify and the solutions they propose. Extend the activity by adding birthday candle holders, candles and decorations. Discuss how these can be shared fairly between the cakes and biscuits.

High rise, low rise

Together, explore ideas about doubling and halving by building on children's interest in constructing tall towers. Encourage the group to use hollow boxes to build as tall a tower as possible. When they have finished, talk about using the same number of blocks to build two towers instead of one. How many blocks in the first tower? Use half the blocks to make a low rise tower – how many blocks then?

Let the children explore making high rise and low rise blocks independently. Talk to them as they halve the number of blocks used. What happens if there are 12 blocks to start? What about 13? If they are confident halving the first number of blocks, can they do it again, for example, half of 12 blocks is 6 blocks; half of 6 blocks is 3 blocks. What is half of 3 blocks?

Tall towers

Provide some blocks or empty boxes that are not very easy to stack. Ask one child to build a tower – this could be three, four or five blocks tall. Count the blocks together. How many blocks would you need to make two towers of the same height? Talk to the children about 'doubling'. If one tower uses five blocks, how many do two towers use?

Extend the problem for older children and when they are confident with 'teens' and numbers to 20, support them as they explore towers of eight, nine or ten blocks.

The role of the adult

The best problems for children are those that they identify themselves. They also need opportunities to problem solve together. One of the key roles of practitioners is to develop situations in which children can refine their problem-solving skills and apply their growing number knowledge to the situations at hand.

There are many opportunities to investigate and solve problems throughout the learning provision that you make for children. The type of support and experiences they need in order to become maths problem solvers include:

- **Lots of maths talk and discussion.**

  Language is part of maths learning because talking problems through is vital. Encourage discussion through enabling statements and open questions.

- **Hands-on solving problem activities across all areas of the setting.**

  Children learn maths through all their experiences and therefore need to take part in creative and interesting activities to get the most maths from those activities.

- **Opportunities for working with numbers up to 20 in a problem-solving situation with particular emphasis on understanding the relationships between the numbers up to ten.**

- **Practical experience of using measuring skills and knowledge about shape and space to solve problems.**

Investigating 'I wonder how many spots there are altogether on a 1 to 6 dice'.

Maths home challenges

Just a minute

Just how long is a minute? We often say 'in a minute', but what do we mean?

Run around outside for exactly one minute.

Did that feel like a short time?
Or did it feel like a long time?

Now sit still for a minute.

Did that feel like a short time? Or did it feel like a long time?

Did it feel longer or shorter than when you were running around?

Try out some other things that you can do for a minute.

Have fun!

Who sank the boat?

Collect together a selection of empty containers which float, such as cheese containers and margarine tubs, to use as boats. Find some pebbles, conkers and other small objects that you could load onto the boats.

Put some water in a bowl or basin and float your 'boats'. Find out how many of the small objects you can load into a boat before it sinks.

What happens if you change the boat or you change the loading objects – does the boat still sink?

Have fun!

Looking for numbers

Collect ten coins and examine them carefully to see whether you can see any numbers on them. If you can, write down the numbers .

Write down any other numbers that you can see in the room.

Have you looked to see whether there are any numbers on the television, on the CD player or on the radio?

Are there numbers on the washing machine? What about the telephone or the microwave oven?

What's the largest number you can find?

Have fun!

Collecting and sorting

Collections of interesting boxes are great to explore and to collect things in.

As adults, we often find ourselves sorting things in real situations, whether it is the post – junk mail, bills or important letters; the shopping when we return from the shops, or the washing – hot wash, cool wash or dry cleaning? But do adults include children in these everyday tasks – sorting socks or putting tins away – or have we forgotten the importance of carrying these out in partnership with children, allowing them to act as apprentices to household tasks?

When considering the ways in which children learn mathematics, it is worth reflecting on our own childhood. When we were young…

- **What did we play?**

- **Where did we play?**

- **Who did we play with?**

- **How did we know when it was time to go home?**

Many of the activities engaged in and the games played involved so much mathematics, and a lot of collecting and sorting. For many of us, 'collections' in childhood were just 'something we did', whether it included conkers, marbles, stamps, coins or stickers.

As adults, we need to build and capitalize on this fascination to support learning. Many of the collections we provide for children in schools and settings are multi-coloured plastic 'sorting sets' purchased from educational catalogues, and these can often be sterile and uninspiring. Practitioners who really 'tune into' children know that the way to extend their learning is to build on their current interests and learning needs.

Developing collections is a really positive way to involve families too. You could start with a parental workshop based around collecting and sorting, and share the beginnings of some collections, inviting donations. Ask families what their children are interested in – you might be surprised. If families are involved in the collections, they will have shared ownership and are far more likely to engage with suggested activities.

Collecting

Of course, all early years' settings have collections of basic resources which children will use across areas of provision indoors and outdoors. These include:

- **small world play wild animals, farm animals, dinosaurs, sea creatures, minibeasts, people**

- **model cars, trucks, trains, boats, planes, helicopters**

- **funnels, bottles, jugs, containers, tubes, bowls**

- **large and small wooden blocks, plastic bricks, hollow blocks, logs**

It is important that practitioners maintain these collections, and that children have ready access to these to support their learning. In addition to these, however, it is essential that specific collections are developed to support children's learning in general and mathematical learning in particular.

What sort of objects are good starting points for these collections? The most obvious answer is those which lead to sorting in a variety of ways. You know the children you work with best, but it is highly likely that they will begin by sorting according to colour. Often this will be because of their previous experiences, perhaps based on interactions with adults who often seem disproportionately preoccupied with matching and naming colours. Children will often naturally sort by size – on a plate of home-made cakes or biscuits they very quickly sort into the 'biggest' and the 'smallest', and have a very strong feeling of what is 'fair' and what isn't.

It is important that practitioners help children organize collections in a systematic way. For example, provide hooks for aprons, cups and sand and water play resources; outlines of collections to support investigations, including magnifiers and containers; partitioned trays; coloured felt or carpet squares; sorting circles or egg boxes/bun trays for impromptu collections. This will lead to a lot of talk about collections and children will begin to understand that when things are organized systematically, counting and manipulating numbers is far easier.

The following collections make a good start for any setting, and can be supplemented to reflect children's current interests and fascinations:

- **socks**
- **locks and keys**
- **boxes**
- **natural objects**
- **balls and spheres**
- **bags and purses**
- **coins**
- **necklaces and beads**
- **snakes**
- **buttons**
- **bottles**

Children collect things spontaneously, and the beginnings of collections are brought into settings, e.g. pebbles, leaves, seashells, fir cones or conkers. Interesting collections give children opportunities to explore descriptive and comparative vocabulary, and it is important that practitioners identify and model the use of specific vocabulary. Wherever possible, vocabulary should be shared with families so that the same words are being used at home and in the setting. If children are using words such as 'soft', 'smooth', 'shiny' and 'hard' to describe objects, introduce more descriptive vocabulary, such as: pliable, malleable, flexible, spongy, bendable, elastic, silky, downy, velvety, glossy, firm, solid, stiff, rigid, tough, durable, inflexible, gleaming, polished, sparkly, glittery, reflective or burnished.

Encourage children's natural desire to collect by providing interesting containers to collect things in – as a rule of thumb, if you want children to collect big things, provide big bags, boxes or containers; if you want them to collect small things, provide small bags, boxes and containers. Families and friends are a great source of reclaimed bags and boxes – try asking them before the Christmas holidays to collect all shiny and interesting gift bags, tins and boxes, and then store these centrally. Consider making simple bags with handles using interesting textured and patterned fabric and start a collection of wooden boxes, which can be developed over time.

Encourage children to make collections in shiny bags.

Collecting— experiences and activities

Scavenger search

Provide each child with a shiny gift bag and go on a scavenger hunt – start with a short walk within the setting's grounds and move to the wider local environment on another occasion. Encourage the children to collect interesting objects in their bag. Take the opportunity to sit down outdoors and take turns to describe the items. Back inside, display the collections and share the descriptive vocabulary.

Teeny weeny objects

Give each child an A4 piece of card, with a strip of double-sided tape fixed down the centre. Encourage children to find small things to fix to the card – be clear about the 'rules' before the search and ensure children know this doesn't include any living creatures! Talk about the things children have found – are they parts of things? How big is the whole leaf likely to be? If there are several parts of one thing, how do they fit together?

Buried treasure

Hide gems, coins, gold nuggets, necklaces, rings and other treasure in the dry sand tray. Provide sieves for children to sift for buried treasure to place in their own 'treasure chests'. How many can they find at once? Who has the most? Which is the longest necklace? Which is the biggest jewel?

Dinosaur hunt

Hide a collection of large plastic dinosaurs in the outdoor area. Provide photographic images of all the missing creatures and send the children on a 'dinosaur hunt'. As each dinosaur is found, match it to the image until all are recovered. Support children as they hide the dinosaurs for others to find. Can they give their friends hints, using positional language?

Sunflowers

This growing experience can take place over more than one term. Begin by sorting a collection of sunflower seeds, then grow the sunflowers, using standard and non-standard measures to record their growth. Finally, harvest the sunflower heads and investigate the collection of flowers. Talk about the size, colour, shape and patterns of the flowers. Could anything else that is similar be added to the collection?

Kim's game

Create a collection of interesting objects with the children. Explore the objects and talk about them together. Lay all the items on a tray, cover them with a cloth and then hide one item behind your back. The children have to guess which item is missing – if no one knows, offer hints. With young children, start the game with six objects; with older children or those who are familiar with the game, use more objects. Extend the game by removing more than one item at a time.

What's in the bag?

Make a small collection of objects and talk about them with the children. Put all the items in a bag, then ask the children to take turns to feel one thing at a time, and describe it for everyone else to identify. When the children are familiar with the activity, make it part of a routine, with children providing objects and giving each other hints.

Matching objects

Create digital images of familiar objects and provide both these and the physical objects for children to investigate and discuss. Encourage the children to match the real object with the photographic image. Extend the activity by providing images of just part of the object – which bear does the image of the leg belong too? Whose nose is it?

Stacking and nesting

Younger children are often fascinated with items of different sizes that stack or nest – Russian matryoshka dolls, stacking beakers or interesting boxes. Support the children as they sequence the objects and then fit them together. Where appropriate, model the use of ordinal numbers.

Bug breakfast

Use a collection of plastic minibeasts as the focus for a calculating activity. Count the number of bugs in the collection as you 'feed' them to a large soft toy/puppet frog with an opening mouth (a zipped mouth is even better). Remove some bugs and count them with the children. If there are ten bugs altogether, and five are still in the basket, how many has the frog eaten? Support the children as they use the frog and the bugs independently.

Big and bigger

Provide a collection of large, empty cardboard boxes and lengths of fabric. Observe the children to see how they use the collection – how do they fit items together? What do they construct? What mathematical language are they using?

Noisy tins

Display a variety of interesting small objects in wicker baskets, e.g. pebbles, shells, conkers, buttons and beads. Encourage the children to put objects into the tins: What sort of noises do they make? Can they guess what is in each tin? Can they tell what sort of object is in the tin? How many objects are in the tin? How can they remember the contents of each tin?

What's in the box?

Collect eight identical boxes and four sets of identical objects. Place one set of objects in each box. Children take turns to open two boxes. If they find a pair, they keep the boxes. If no pair is found, the boxes are replaced and the next child takes a turn to open two more boxes. The game continues until all the pairs are found. Older children can play the game with more boxes and objects, or with images of objects.

Bits and pieces

Give the children opportunities to explore a variety of small items, such as beads, buttons or coins – support them as they line the objects up, or make a pattern or array. Consider adding empty chocolate box or biscuit trays. Model the use of mathematical vocabulary.

Sorting

Sorting activities, starting with real objects, offer children opportunities to think mathematically, and develop visual discrimination and descriptive language. They also link very closely with shape recognition (chapter 3), counting (chapter 1) and calculating (chapter 2). Practical, dynamic sorting activities give children opportunities to record using real objects and this forms a firm foundation for using information and handling data in later years.

Experiences for children are always more meaningful if they are relevant and real. There are lots of 'real life' activities in settings which involve sorting, for example, 'tidy-up time'. This can become a chaotic affair, particularly when a large number of new children who have not experienced a managed 'tidy up' before join a group. However, the routine of the day can be turned into a real mathematical learning experience – with pairs or small groups of children taking responsibility for organizing areas of provision, sorting items and returning them to the correct collection (set). This is the ideal opportunity to discuss meaningfully items which are 'wild animals' or 'not wild animals' – and if they are not wild animals, what are they – farm animals, dinosaurs, puppets?

It is vital that practitioners are aware of children's development in sorting and can plan progression for activities. During the early stages, it is important that when children are exploring a group of objects, they can talk about what is the same about the items, and what is different. They need to be able to identify which objects belong in one particular set, and which don't – for example 'cars' and 'not cars'. Children need lots of opportunities to sort using their own criteria, before sorting for a reason identified by an adult. This was very clearly illustrated when I asked a child to find two socks that had something 'the same' about them. The two socks selected couldn't have been more different – in size, colour, pattern and fabric. I simply could not see what the similarity was, until I asked. The response 'my sister has both of them' indicates a very personal sorting criterion – without this it would have been very easy to have noted that the child didn't understand the meaning of 'the same'.

Children often progress naturally to sorting into two or more sets, so the emphasis moves from 'car' or 'not car' to 'car or boat' or 'car, boat or train'.

Later, children move to sorting and resorting. This may involve finding similarities in a set which has already been sorted. For example, if you sort the children into two groups using your own criteria, can they then identify the criteria used, possibly blue socks and not blue socks? Children also move to sorting into more than one set – sorting a collection of vehicles into first a set of cars and a set of trucks and then resorting the original collection into a set of blue vehicles and a set of red vehicles. Some children find sorting by more than one property quite a challenge, for example, from a collection of vehicles, finding all the red cars, or all the blue trains.

Older children can begin to use simple sorting diagrams with real objects, e.g. Venn or Carroll diagrams. The simplest Carroll diagram (named after Lewis Carroll) is often used to group things according to yes/no. For instance, two squares drawn onto card, labelled with a tick and a cross to represent being a 'car' or 'not a car' could be used to create a simple Carroll diagram. A simple Venn diagram can be created using two overlapping sorting circles – vehicles can be sorted into 'red' and 'cars' and the overlapping intersection of the two sets contains 'red cars'.

Create an 'investigations' table and add new, intriguing objects to investigate and sort.

Sorting— experiences and activities

Splash!

Fill the water tray with clear water and place two baskets labelled 'float' and 'sink' nearby. Provide a variety of objects and ask children to predict which objects will float and which will sink, then test their hypothesis for one object at a time. When the object has been tested children should decide which basket it belongs in. Will the metal boat float or sink? Which set has the most objects in it? When the children have finished, provide fishing nets for children to catch items and use their own criteria to sort.

Socks

Make a collection of socks in a laundry basket, making sure to include some interesting pairs such as walking socks, bed socks, booties, football socks, socks of different sizes. Provide a washing line at child height with lots of pegs. Encourage children to choose two socks and talk about something that is the same and something that is different about them. After discussing the socks, can the children find all the pairs? How quickly can they peg them up?

Gloves

Supply a selection of assorted gloves, including 'magic' gloves which stretch when filled. Put them in the dry sand, with spoons and funnels. Can the children find matching pairs to fill? What is different when they are full compared to when they are empty?

Sort me out

Create an investigation area for sorting – provide a different collection every week. Consider: things with holes, things that stretch, wooden things, shiny things, things that make a noise, things with wheels. Provide trays, baskets and clear containers to sort things into. Encourage children to select their own criteria to sort and explain what they have done. Use speech bubbles to record children's comments and display these in the area, with photos of the sets.

Odd one out

Offer children a basket of objects and ask them to identify the 'odd one out' – try a selection of pebbles and stones and a twig. Ask the children to explain the reason for their choice. Extend the activity by providing three or four baskets, each with an odd item. When all the 'odd ones out' have been found, can the children make a new collection with a new 'odd one'? As the children become more confident, place the objects in a feely bag – can they find the ball in a set of cubes or a car in a set of animals?

Same and different

Make a collection of head scarves and patterned handkerchiefs available in a wicker basket. Encourage the children to explore the squares of fabric and talk about similarities and differences. Each child takes a turn to select two squares and identify something that is the same about them, and something that is different. With older children, extend the activity so that the child identifies one similarity between the objects and the other children have to guess what it is.

Moo, grunt, neigh

Enhance small-world farm play to include fields with fences clearly labelled with pictures or words. Draw children's attention to these and encourage them to sort animals into the correct field, e.g. cows, horses, sheep, pigs. All animals which don't belong in any of the fields (sets) stay outside the pens. Talk to children about the contents of the sets and what is the same and what is different about them, for example, do all animals have four legs?

Sort and resort

Fill a biscuit tin with several objects that can be sorted in different ways, for example, some items that go in the water, some items with wheels and some animals. Ask one child to sort the items using their own criteria. This could be 'vehicles' and 'not vehicles', meaning, for example, that a boat would be with the train and cars. The other children have to guess the criteria used. When everyone is sure, the child reveals their criteria. Then, mix the objects up and ask another child to sort them. This time, the boat may be with 'things that go in the water', including a fish and a dolphin, rather than with the other vehicles which would be in the set 'things that do not go in the water'.

Carroll diagrams

Draw a thick black line down the centre of a piece of A1 card. Talk to the children about the diagram – one side is the positive aspect of the sort, for example 'red' or 'wood'; the other is the negative aspect of the sort – 'not red' or 'not wood'. Encourage the children to choose a way of sorting and placing items on the diagram using their own criteria, for example, spotty or not spotty, edible or not edible. Older children can use simple drawings to record their diagram.

Trying it on

Give children lots of time to explore a collection of clothes, including hats, trousers, gloves, boots, coats, in different fabrics, some for winter and some for summer. Ask two children to find things which fulfil a specific criterion and put them on – who can find the most and put them on quickest? For example, 'things that come in pairs' or 'things we only wear outdoors'. When all the correct clothes are on, talk about the positive and negative properties – 'things that come in pairs' (gloves and boots) and 'things that don't come in pairs' (hats and coats). Do trousers really come in pairs?

More than one

When children are very familiar with sorting by one attribute (property), they will begin to sort by two attributes. Select items carefully, so that they can be clear about the process and can talk about it. For example, provide circles and squares in four colours. Ask the children to find shapes which are square and blue. When they have found items that are both blue and square, support one child to set a challenge for others, e.g. 'I challenge Rima to find a red circle'. As the children gain confidence, try sorting by three attributes – what challenges can they set for each other?

Venn diagrams

Place a variety of interesting items in a circle on the ground outdoors. Place two plastic hoops, overlapping, next to this collection of objects. Place three items in the diagram: one in each circle, and one in the intersection – for example, a red ball in one circle, a car in the second circle, and a red car in the intersection. Ask a child to choose another item and place it in the Venn diagram. If the item isn't red, or a car, it stays outside the diagram. Extend the activity by inviting children to provide labels for the different collections that have been sorted.

Collections

Collections throughout the provision, including the maths workshop area

Maths learning should take place throughout the provision, not only during activities that focus on mathematics, or that occur in the mathematics learning zone or maths workshop area (sometimes called the maths reference area). However, every learning environment needs an area as a base for maths storage, so that adults and children know where specific resources to support maths learning are available. In addition to resources to support exploration of measures, this learning zone should include a variety of objects for sorting, classifying, ordering and counting. These will include:

- shells, pebbles and rocks

- conkers, fir cones and twigs

- wooden and plastic 2D and 3D shapes

- pegs, buttons, beads and threading shapes

- cotton reels

- ribbons and decorative tape

- ties

- sorting circles, coloured mats, sorting trays, coloured card

- tins, boxes, gift bags, baskets

- animals, cars, people

- linking objects

- cubes, blocks, bricks

In addition, children need regular access to games, including:

- counting

- shape matching

- colour matching

- track games

- lotto – picture, shape, photo, colour, number

- snap – picture, shape, photo, colour, number

- dominoes – picture, shape, photo, colour, number, texture

- board and card games

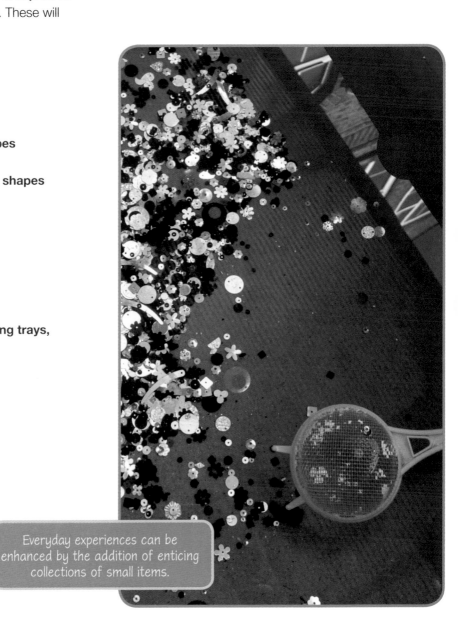

Everyday experiences can be enhanced by the addition of enticing collections of small items.

Imaginative role play and collections

Role play and home-corner play are essential areas in every early years setting, and as such, are part of the core provision available every day. However, these are sometimes the most difficult areas to maintain. One very effective way to ensure these areas remain vibrant and interesting for young children is to limit what is available at all times to a minimum of high-quality resources that can be used in a number of ways. These resources can then be revisited and enhanced on a regular basis, to support children's current interests and enthusiasms.

The following are ideas for collections to enhance the home corner and role play areas:

Develop a **florist shop** indoors and a complementary garden centre role-play area outdoors, and add the following to enhance the home corner:

* silk flowers in pots and vases

* watering cans and plant sprayers

* window boxes

* flower pots

* small garden forks and trowels

* individual silk flowers, gift wrap and ribbons

* gardening gloves

Develop a **veterinary surgery** indoors, a pet-rescue team outdoors and add the following to enhance the home corner:

▲ a pet puppy soft toy or puppet

▲ dog biscuits and bones

▲ vet appointment diary

▲ empty dog food tins and packets

▲ carry box and dog bed

▲ dog collar and lead

▲ timetable for walks, food and medicine

Develop a **post office** indoors, parcel delivery service outdoors and add the following to enhance the home corner:

■ envelopes and writing paper

■ postcards

■ address books

■ stamps

■ invitations, thank-you cards and birthday cards

■ order forms

■ brown wrapping paper, sticky tape, string

Develop a **clothes store** or launderette indoors, washing and washing line outdoors and add the following to enhance the home corner:

★ laundry basket

★ empty washing powder boxes

★ empty fabric softener bottles and boxes

★ pairs of socks

★ baby clothes and children's clothes

★ instructions for washing machine

★ timer

Making matching games

Lotto

Young children need lots of time to explore and investigate collections of interesting items. At the same time, they will be playing simple matching games including 'snap', 'lotto' and 'dominoes'. It is very easy to combine these two interests and support the children to make their own lotto games.

Lotto games have a very simple formula – generally six pictures on each of four base boards for younger children (increasing to eight or nine pictures for older children), with each of the pictures on the base boards duplicated on individual cards (making twenty-four in a basic set). Once children are familiar with the rules of the game, talk to them about the sorts of things they would like to see in their own lotto game – this will often be themselves, or familiar things around the setting. Support children as they make digital images themselves – each child could make just one, or small groups could each take several photographs, to make more than one lotto game.

Then print out copies of two sets of images, six to a sheet. Keep four of each set as the base boards, and cut the duplicate set into 24 individual cards. Where possible, laminate the cards and base boards for durability.

These lotto games can be used within the setting, or individual sets can be taken home to share with family and friends. Ensure those using the game are familiar with the rules and the vocabulary that can be introduced and modelled.

As children gain confidence making these lotto games, encourage them to make the game more difficult by adding similar objects – for example, three different sorts of puppets or three different balls. How can they describe these to each other before sharing the card?

The base boards for lotto can be used in different ways too – can the children make a collection of all the real objects in the images? This is a good way to move children from the use of real objects, to photographic images and later to pictures or diagrams.

Dominoes

This formula for making a set of dominoes can be used to make small dominoes for indoor use, or large dominoes for use outdoors. The principle is always the same – you need **seven** different panels.

Ideas for domino sets – large or small:

- colours, shapes or patterns
- textures
- photographs – of children, animals, places or theme-related
- numerals

To create a set of patterned dominoes

You need:

- patterned paper (wrapping paper is ideal) in seven different patterns.

To make 28 A4-sized dominoes:

1. Cut seven pieces of A5-sized paper for each different pattern.

2.. Choose the first pattern and glue it to one half of seven A4 cards. Then stick one piece of each of the other patterns to the other half.

3. Continue until you have 28 different dominoes. If you need more guidance, look at a set of commercially-produced colour or number dominoes.

For example, if your seven patterns are: stripes, spots, checks, stars, circles, zigzags and squares, the dominoes will be as follows:

stripes	spots	spots	checks
stripes	checks	spots	stars
stripes	stars	spots	circles
stripes	circles	spots	zigzags
stripes	zigzags	spots	squares
stripes	squares	spots	spots
stripes	stripes		
checks	stars	stars	circles
checks	circles	stars	zigzags
checks	zigzags	stars	squares
checks	squares	stars	stars
checks	checks		
circles	zigzags	zigzags	squares
circles	squares	zigzags	zigzags
circles	circles	squares	squares

4. Laminate the A4 cards for durability.

The role of the adult

Many young children naturally collect objects, even if they start by putting them in their pockets, or filling up the handbags in the home corner. It is essential that practitioners build on this fascination and also inspire other children to make and explore collections. Children need to see adults making and using collections and sorting in different ways for real purposes. It is important to help children to make connections when they are collecting and sorting – if they have a collection in a bag, box or container that they want to count and are finding it difficult, help them to think of an easier way. If they don't think of making a line of objects, suggest it to them.

Practitioners need to plan:

✦ **to enrich all areas of provision to support collecting and sorting**

✦ **activities that promote sorting and collecting**

✦ **to introduce and model the use of the vocabulary which is important to these experiences.**

The following experiences and activities particularly help children understand about collecting and sorting:

• **pretend play with objects that can be sorted in different ways, e.g. cars and trucks, animals, dolls**

• **using a range of creative materials**

• **exploring exciting collections of everyday objects, e.g. ties, gloves, socks, fruit**

• **making collections of things outdoors in large boxes and bags**

• **tidying up, sorting objects into the right trays and boxes**

• **talking about things that are the same and things that are different**

• **playing with matching games and making their own**

• **using diverse containers indoors to sort and collect items, e.g. bags, boxes, tins, purses**

Enriching provision

By creating a mathematics workshop you will be providing children with a base where a wide variety of collections of resources can be stored. These can be used by children to support their learning throughout the areas of provision, both indoors and outdoors.

Collections of appropriate resources across areas of provision will also support children's explorations and investigations. Children need access to high-quality small world resources to support their imaginative pretend play: wooden and plastic furniture to sort into rooms in a dolls' house; farm and wild animals to sort into fields; trucks and cars to collect and move around car mats, car parking spaces and garages; assorted cats to put into boxes. The creative area gives children opportunities to add to collections (e.g. where do the tubes and small boxes belong?) or to use collections, e.g. sorting fabrics by colour, shape or size.

Tidy-up time can be a fantastic learning experience for children if resources are stored in clearly marked trays, boxes, sacks and jars. Try pairing children who are confident at sorting and returning items independently with children who need more support. Can one group of children sort the pens, pencils and markers in the mark-making area before the sand and water toys have been sorted, or the musical instruments returned to the correct boxes?

What could be more appealing than sorting a bowl of treasure?

Essential collecting and sorting vocabulary

Introduce, model and reinforce the use of specific mathematical vocabulary such as:

- The same as
- Different from
- Big, bigger, biggest
- Small, smaller, smallest
- Bigger than, smaller than
- Taller than, shorter than
- 1, 2, 3, 4 . . .

- 1st, 2nd, 3rd, 4th . . .
- Less/least, more/most
- Few, fewer, fewest
- Enough/ not enough
- Sort, set, group, share
- Graph, chart, list

- Row, line them up
- Altogether
- How many more?
- Is the same as

Open-ended questions and enabling statements about collecting and sorting

I wonder why this stone is with the smooth pebbles..?

What can you tell me about your favourite animal?

I think this fir cone belongs with the twigs.

Can you explain why you think the tallest dinosaur is Rashid's favourite?

What is the same about those two socks? What is different?

My favourite flower is the biggest yellow one.

Maybe that glove could be with this one... What can we say about the treasure?

I haven't got any animals in my collection. I wonder what I could have..?

What did you notice about the collection of seashells?

Maths home challenges

Collections

With this week's challenge you will find a small plastic container.

Talk to your child about the sorts of things which will fit in the container.

Make a collection of tiny things together and see how many will fit inside the container – 1, 2, 3 or more?

Talk about things that are the same about the objects – for example, they are all small!

Talk about the things that are different – the colour, what they are used for, are they soft or hard?

Bring the container and some of the items that fit inside it back here so that we can all share and talk about them.

Have fun!

Collecting and sorting

Collect five things which belong in the bathroom, for example:

- sponge
- soap
- toothbrush
- hairbrush
- toothpaste

Collect five things which belong in the kitchen, for example:

- wooden spoon
- dish brush
- mug
- plastic bowl
- egg cup

Spread out three hand towels on the floor.

Put all the objects onto one of the towels, and take some time to look at them and talk about them.

Now begin to sort them into two groups – you could start with 'bathroom things' and 'kitchen things'.

Take turns to put each item into one group and say why it belongs there.

Shoes and socks

Ask your child to collect as many shoes and socks as possible.

How many pairs can you find together?

Talk about the shoes and the socks, then each choose two different items.

Say one thing that is the same about the two things.

Take turns until you cannot think of anything else that is the same.

Now start to talk about things that are different!

Words and phrases to use:

- The same as
- Different from
- More than
- Less than

Have fun!

Stories and rhymes

Contemporary rhymes support counting backwards and forwards.

Some early years practitioners love exploring maths with young children and feel very able to take children on in their maths learning journey. Others feel less confident in supporting children with maths and sometimes books and rhymes can be a great way into maths for both adults and children together.

We all know that talk about mathematics is vital in supporting children's growing understanding. Before the age of 7, children mainly use words that parents and other adults use with them in their conversations (Biemiller, 2003). We also know that the number of words heard by children impacts clearly on their vocabulary which in turn impacts on literacy development (Hart and Risley, 1995).

Books are valuable for introducing mathematical vocabulary in an exciting, fun and non-threatening way. The national 'Every Child a Talker' programme identified many strategies for practitioners and families to support children's vocabulary development through books, stories and rhymes, including dialogic book talk. With dialogic book talk, children and adults have a real conversation about the book. Sharing the book is a two-way process

– the adult becomes a listener, a questioner and an audience for the child and the child becomes the teller of the story. This means that lots of time must be allowed to discuss the text and the pictures, focusing on the child's chosen pages, rather than racing to the end of the book. Remember that books don't have to be labelled 'maths books' to support children's maths learning – mathematical themes run through many beloved books and stories and practitioners must identify and build on this.

Number rhymes can be used to support maths and are an excellent starting point for engaging families in their children's learning. Can you remember the rhymes you learned as a child? Many adults have fond memories of sharing much-loved songs and rhymes while sitting close to a trusted adult – but not all children have opportunities to share rhymes at home. Children's mathematical understanding can be developed through number rhymes and songs and linked to imaginative play. What could be more fun than pretending to be a 'speckled frog' or a 'little duck', wearing a favourite hat or mask?

Traditional stories

Many children come to early years settings with experiences of hearing traditional stories – those read or told by family members, or animated versions from DVDs. It is essential to develop these familiar home experiences and draw out the maths elements in the tales. Some stories focus on specific numbers of characters: *The Three Little Pigs*, *The Wolf and the Seven Little Kids*, *Goldilocks and the Three Bears* and *The Three Billy Goats Gruff* (also size). Other books explore size in particular: *Cinderella*, *The Elves and the Shoemaker*, *Jack and the Beanstalk* and *The Enormous Turnip*. Lots of traditional tales include journeys, for example, *Snow White and the Seven Dwarves*, *Hansel and Gretel*, *Stone Soup* and *The Gingerbread Man*.

It is important that children hear the stories being read and told, as well as having time to revisit, retell, act out and innovate, for example – new endings (Goldilocks stays in the forest or the wolf makes friends with the pigs); new characters (the five little fish building underwater homes or the enormous carrot), or new settings (getting lost in the jungle or on the moon). Practitioners need to develop story props which support the maths in traditional stories, for example, lots of shoes and shoe boxes to retell *The Elves and the Shoemaker* and magnetic props of the *Three Billy Goats Gruff* or the Three Bears to support children in their retelling of stories.

Of course, traditional tales often include elements of fantasy and magic too, and practitioners should capitalize on some children's fascination with this – can they create recipes for potions and magical spells?

Traditional stories engage children and offer opportunities to talk about all aspects of mathematics.

Traditional stories – experiences and activities

Goldilocks and the three bears

Set up an interactive display on a picnic blanket. Include three bears of different sizes, and add three bowls and spoons of different sizes too. Remember to include an empty porridge box and a copy of the story *Goldilocks and the Three Bears*. Observe what children do and say as they interact with the display, and scribe their comments in speech bubbles to add to it. Extend the activity by giving children opportunities to make or decorate chairs of different sizes for the bears.

Building houses for the three little pigs

Give the children opportunities to explore making houses for the three little pigs in the creative workshop – using straw, twigs and blocks. Develop the building with bricks and blocks by providing soft toy pigs of different sizes – can the children choose the right materials to make a house for one pig, two pigs, or all three pigs? Move the activity outside and support children in making houses for the pigs that they can fit inside – use A-frames, broomsticks set in concrete in buckets, lengths of fabric and large empty cardboard boxes.

Billy Goats Gruff story box

Make a *Three Billy Goats Gruff* story box with the children. Use a shoe box and cut down one side to make a stage. Include some fake grass, some shiny blue fabric, natural objects such as pebbles, cones, twigs and grass, three goats of different sizes, a troll and some blocks to make a bridge. Reinforce the use of descriptive language and support the children as they retell the story. Extend the activity by making magnetic story props using the children's drawings.

The elves and the shoemaker

When the children are familiar with the story, provide assorted pairs of slippers, shoes and boots, and boot boxes of different sizes (shoe shops are often happy to provide empty boxes). Encourage the children to try the footwear on and then fit their feet into the boxes. Are the shoes too big? Is the box too small?

Stories are a great starting point for active, hands-on experiences about size and numbers.

Magic beans

Focus on the magic beans from *Jack and the Beanstalk*, using the magic beans instead of dice. Children play in pairs – each child has a collection of treasure items, with more treasure in a treasure chest. Taking turns, each child throws five beans, counting how many land gold-side up. The child then has to decide whether to add or subtract from their treasure collection. So if Max has seven items, will he add three items, or take away three items? Focus on talking about what is happening and why.

The enormous turnip

Discuss the story of the enormous turnip. Retell the story with children taking the role of the characters, starting with the tallest child and ending with the shortest child, taking on the role of the mouse. Remember to fall down when the turnip is pulled up. Supply a real turnip, and lots of possible characters from the story. Support the children as they order the characters by size and retell their own versions of the story.

The giant pumpkin

Giant fruit and vegetables make a great starting point for exploring size. Provide a pumpkin for each small group of children. Which is the biggest? Or the heaviest? How can they find out? Use non-standard measures to measure the pumpkin and talk about the best way of finding out the size and weight. Can the children put their arms all the way around the pumpkin, or is it too big? Help the children to scoop the flesh out of the pumpkins and find the seeds. How can they estimate how many seeds there are? Which pumpkin has the most seeds?

Consider making pumpkin soup with the children (see opposite).

Ingredients:

- 1/2 pumpkin (peeled and seeded)

- 2 tablespoons butter

- 1 medium onion, chopped

- 3 glasses of water

- nutmeg

- salt and black pepper

- 4 tablespoons of double cream

Method:

Step 1: Boil the pumpkin chunks in water using a microwave or hob.

Step 2: In a pan, fry the onion in butter until golden brown.

Step 3: Mash the boiled pumpkin chunks in the same water with a spoon and add the fried onions and nutmeg. Bring it to the boil.

Step 4: When the soup is cooked, stir in the cream and seasoning to taste.

Moving like this

Talk about characters from traditional stories – giants, elves, fairies, pixies, ogres, princesses, golden geese or rats. How do these creatures move? Try taking giant strides, or tiny pixie footsteps. When the children are confident with ways of moving, mark out 'homes' on the ground with chalk – a castle, a cottage, a forest and a palace. Call out a way of moving, and the children move like a giant or a goose, for example, to music. When the music stops, call out 'house', 'palace', 'castle' or 'forest' and the children have to move to the correct location.

Maths story maps

Use children's natural story-telling talents and their knowledge of traditional tales to make up a story together. Choose a main character and plan and draw a journey together. Remember to add challenges and resolutions, just like a journey in a traditional tale. For example: Once upon a time there was a small girl called Sami. She was going to a picnic with her cousin, so she packed her picnic basket. She took: five cheese rolls, four apples, three packets of crisps, two sausages and one bottle of water. On the way she met not one, not two, but three tiny hungry mice. The mice were so, so hungry – what did Sami do? Later, Sami needed to go across the bridge, but there was a huge, fierce dog. What did Sami do next?

Be sure to focus on the number of items, and remember to talk about the maths in the story – if Sami had five cheese rolls and she gave one to the hungry mice, how many were left? If Sami swops one apple for two cherries, how many pieces of fruit does she have altogether?

Gingerbread man

Make brown uncooked play dough (not to be eaten!) with the children, adding mixed spiced for authenticity.

Ingredients:

- 2 cups flour

- 2 cups warm water

- 1 cup salt

- 2 tablespoons vegetable oil

- 1 tablespoon cream of tartar

Method:

Step 1: Mix all the ingredients together and knead until smooth.

Step 2: Provide assorted gingerbread men cutters, and small beads, buttons and sequins for decoration.

Alternatively, make a salt dough cooked gingerbread man, add a wolf puppet and other characters from the story and support the children as they retell the tale.

Core rhymes

Traditional and contemporary rhymes play a key role in supporting children's early literacy and numeracy development, but some children enter settings knowing only one or two rhymes, or sometimes, none at all.

The Bookstart Survey (2009) revealed that the UK is falling out of love with nursery rhymes, with parents claiming that nursery rhymes are simply too old-fashioned to interest their children. Just over a third of parents surveyed regularly used nursery rhymes with their children, while almost a quarter admitted that they had never sung a nursery rhyme with their child. What's more, a third of young parents surveyed (16–24) said that nursery rhymes were too old-fashioned while 20 per cent claimed that they were not educational enough to use with their children. Just over half of men surveyed knew all the words to the nation's favourite rhyme – *Twinkle Twinkle Little Star* – compared to 83 per cent of women.

Practitioners in all early years settings use number rhymes, but this can often be in a slightly haphazard way – chanting or singing children's chosen rhymes and songs in a 'lucky dip approach'. A far more systematic approach to using number rhymes to support children's maths development is needed.

Choose a set of 8–10 rhymes, which support both counting on and counting back, and plan to introduce one rhyme each week, finding the opportunity to share the rhyme at each group time. This doesn't mean that other rhymes will not be shared, but the focus for the week will be on one particular rhyme. Develop a box to store all the resources which support each rhyme. So if the focus for the week is *Five Little Ducks*, experiences for the week would include:

- **opportunities to retell the rhyme with magnetic props**

- **sorting a collection of assorted ducks**

- **playing 'catch the duck' with nets in the water**

- **looking at books about ducks and ducklings**

- **matching numbered ducks to numbered lily pads**

- **playing track games about ducks**

By the end of each week, children should be confident with the core rhyme, and as they move on, the collection can be developed. Remember to give children lots of opportunities to make up their own number rhymes too – 'Ten green bottles' on a wall can be easily changed to pink jellyfish, fluffy teddies, barking dogs or fierce monsters.

Baking currant buns together gives children real life experience which can be linked to a favourite rhyme.

Possible core number rhymes

- Five little men in a flying saucer

- Five little speckled frogs

- Five little ducks

- One, two, three, four, five, once I caught a fish alive

- Five little monkeys jumping on the bed

- Five little monkeys and the crocodile

- Ten green bottles

- Ten in a bed

- Ten fat sausages

- One little elephant

- One, two, buckle my shoe

- This old man

- Two little dicky birds

- One man went to mow

Core rhymes — experiences and activities

Number rhyme headbands

1. Make cardboard headbands to fit the children. Fix one half of Velcro to the centre of each headband.

2. Support children as they draw pictures of core number rhymes, including:

    *   ducks
    *   monkeys
    *   frogs
    *   aliens

3. Colour photocopy the pictures.

4. Laminate five pictures and fix the other half of the Velcro to each.

Use laminated colour copies with magnetic tape as magnetic rhyme props too.

Children can wear the headbands on their heads as they actively play out being frogs, ducks or aliens, and chant the rhyme together.

Five speckled frogs and lily pads

Develop a collection of different frogs for children to explore, and try to get families involved in contributing to the collections to support rhymes. Then provide five shiny paper 'lily pads' and five frogs so children can revisit the rhyme. Make a simple game with the children:

1. Use an A1 sheet of card and add four lily pads (one in each corner) and a log in the middle.

2. Stick or draw paper 'rocks' and 'lily leaves' between each lily pad and the log. Make sure there are the same number of rocks or leaves between each pad and the log.

3. Support the children as they devise rules for games to move the frogs from the lily pads to the log – try using magic beans, dice or spinners.

Ten in a bed — cardboard bed

Collect ten different soft toys with the children. Use a cardboard box bed, big enough for all ten toys to fit in. Give the children time to explore the toys and retell the rhyme. Introduce a game in which pairs of children take turns to remove a number of toys from the bed – the second child then has to say how many toys are left in the bed. Support the children as they take individual digital images of each toy and make laminated rhyme props to retell the rhyme independently.

Currant bun lotto

With the children, take photos of six buns, then five, four, three, two and one. Use PowerPoint to make four base boards, each with the six images of groups of buns – you will need to make sure you have four different coloured backgrounds. Make individual cards representing the different numbers of buns, again on the four different coloured backgrounds (24 cards in total). Support the children as they play lotto with the currant bun cards. In this version, they will be matching according to the number of buns and the colour of the background, for example, 'red and six' or 'blue and three'.

Making currant buns

Make currant buns with the children – you can use a traditional yeast recipe, or try this simple recipe:

Ingredients:

* 225g self-raising flour

* 100g margarine

* 100g dried fruit

* 50g caster sugar

* 1 egg

* a little milk

Method:

Step 1: Rub the margarine into the flour, and add the sugar and dried fruit.

Step 2: Mix to a stiff dough with the egg and a little milk.

Step 3: Place rough heaps onto a baking tray and bake at 200°C/gas mark 6 for 10–15 minutes.

When the children have eaten the buns, provide play dough, cutters, baking trays and cake cases and a balance for them to revisit the experience.

Gone fishing

When the children are familiar with the rhyme 'One, two, three, four, five', introduce fishing games in the water tray. Mark numerals on plastic fish with indelible pens. Place a laminated A3 card, with fish shapes containing numerals 1–5, next to the water tray. Provide fishing nets for children to catch the plastic fish and sort them into the correct set. Alternatively, provide baskets for each child and support children to calculate as they catch fish, e.g. to add together the numbers on each fish.

Green bottles on a wall

Fill ten green plastic bottles with water or sand and line them up on a wall. Children take turns to throw three bean bags at the bottles. If they knock down two bottles with the first beanbag, how many bottles are left? If they knock three bottles with the next beanbag, how many are left now?

Encourage children to find ways of recording their score – using real objects, tallies, marks or numerals. Extend the activity with teddies on the wall instead of bottles.

Finger puppets

Each child draws two different 'dicky birds' on card. Cut these out and fix each to a narrow ring of card to make two finger puppets. Retell the rhyme of 'Two little dicky birds', changing the names as appropriate.

Alien small world play

Set up an alien small world play in a black tray – use metallic foil over recycled materials to make a landscape, and glitter in sand to make moon dust. Support children as they explore the small world scenario. Encourage them as they count down to lift off; 'five, four, three, two, one'.

Crocodile crossing

When the children are familiar with the rhyme about the crocodile and the monkeys, introduce this game outdoors. One child is the 'crocodile' and the other children line up facing the crocodile. They chant:

Please Mrs Crocodile

May we cross your golden river?

Mrs (or Mr) Crocodile replies:

Only if you are wearing blue/have brown eyes/have a sister etc.

The children who fulfil the criteria can walk past the crocodile in safety to the other side of the river. The children who don't fulfil the criteria must try to run to the other side of the river without getting caught by the crocodile. Those who are caught, join the crocodile. The game continues until all children are caught or safe, and a new crocodile is chosen.

Ten in a bed

Fold the bottom, narrow edge of an A4 piece of card halfway towards the top, forming a 'pocket'. Provide catalogues with images of toy animals for children to talk about and cut out. Children cut out ten toys each and fit them into the pocket – like toys in a bed. They can design their own repeating pattern for the 'bedspread' or 'duvet cover'. These individual 'Ten in a beds' can be used to support children's independent counting.

Contemporary stories

Picture books are an ideal focus for maths conversations. When planning to use a book as a starting point, identify the theme which runs through the book – it could be fruit and vegetables, with opportunities to explore weight; clothes, which stimulate a discussion about pattern or size; or picnics or parties which inspire talk about number and sharing.

Lots of books focus on animals or teddy bears, so offer lots of opportunities to explore one or two mathematical elements through a whole series of experiences and activities.

Build a comprehensive collection of core books, some of which focus specifically on maths, which children can become familiar and confident with over the period of a year. Consider developing prompts for dialogic book talk for each of these stories, using the following format:

Prepare

- **Make sure you are very familiar with the story.**

- **Consider the kinds of prompts and questions you will use to stimulate thought and talk about the story.**

- **Remember the golden rules: ask open-ended questions; recast and expand what children say.**

- **Before you start, ensure you have thought about: the ways in which children might be able to relate the story to their own lives; the new vocabulary that you will introduce in reading and talking about the story; follow-up experiences and activities to consolidate this vocabulary.**

Some contemporary story books which support aspects of mathematics

Who sank the Boat? by Pamela Allen (Puffin, 1990)

Handa's Surprise by Eileen Browne (Walker, 2006)

Dear Zoo by Rod Campbell (Simon and Schuster, 2005),

The Bad Tempered Ladybird by Eric Carle (Picture Puffin, 2010)

Brown Bear, Brown Bear by Eric Carle (Picture Puffin, 1995)

Aliens Love Underpants by Claire Freedman (Simon and Schuster, 2007),

We're going on a Picnic by Pat Hutchins (Red Fox, 2003),

Kipper's Birthday by Mick Inkpen (Hodder, 2008)

Mrs McTats and Her Houseful of Cats by Alyssa Satin Capucilli (Simon and Schuster, 2003),

Dinosaur Roar! By Henrietta Strickland (Koala Books, 2005)

Contemporary stories – experiences and activities

Fruit kebabs

Use *Handa's Surprise* or *The Very Hungry Caterpillar* as a stimulus to make fresh fruit kebabs. Plan a shopping trip with two or three children to buy fruits – include some exotic or unusual fruits which children may not be familiar with. Take time to explore the fruit, then chop into biteable chunks. Put each fruit into a different bowl – pineapple, kiwi fruit, melon, orange, apple, tangerine, grapes. Each child takes a turn to create a repeating pattern for a kebab, e.g. melon, apple, apple, melon, apple, apple. Where appropriate, extend the activity by asking children to estimate how many segments will be in each tangerine or to draw a repeating pattern before making the kebab.

Box it up

When the children are familiar with the book *Dear Zoo,* provide an assortment of toys and lots of different sized boxes. Encourage the children to explore the boxes, find the best box for each animal and decorate it accordingly – for example, black and white stripes for a zebra.

Patterned pants

Provide lots of pants in different sizes, colours and patterns, in a laundry basket. Support children as they explore the pants, sort them and talk about what they are doing. Record the children's comments in speech bubbles.

Ladybird, ladybird

When the children are familiar with the story of *The Bad Tempered Ladybird*, use the patterns on these delightful creatures as a starting point for calculation. Make a simple ladybird outline on A1 card: be sure to include six legs, head, two antennae and two wings, but do not include spots. Laminate the ladybird. Cut out ten black spots, laminate them and fix blu-tack on the back. Count all ten spots with the children, then support them as they fix some spots to one wing. Count them together and predict how many spots will be on the second wing – the total is always ten.

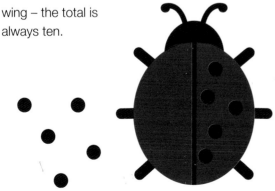

We're Going on a Bear Hunt

Ask the children to draw pictures of the locations visited on the journey taken by the family in *We're Going on a Bear Hunt* – home, grass, water, mud, forest, snowstorm and cave. Fix the pictures onto a huge piece of paper on the ground. Children take turns to program the bee-bot to move from one location to the next – how many moves will it need to make? Does it need to turn right or left? With more experienced children, take turns to give instructions to complete a whole journey from one location to another. Extend the activity with children making their own maps of journeys in other stories.

Acting out favourite tales gives children time and space to explore mathematical concepts.

Making cakes

Add cake-baking tins, teaspoons, silicon or paper cake cases, small moulds, candle holders, candles and plastic cake decorations to the damp sand tray. Put birthday cards for ages 2–7 next to the sand tray. Encourage children to to make 'play cakes'.

Brown Bear, Brown Bear

Using the traditional lotto format and rules for play, make a lotto game with the children based on this book. Use children's black and white drawings photocopied onto coloured sheets, creating four baseboards with six pictures on each. Support the children as they play the game – 'I see a blue dog looking at me', 'I see a purple cat looking at me'. Encourage children to identify what is the same between images and what is different.

Counting cats

Use *Mrs McTats and Her Houseful of Cats* or *My Cat likes to Hide in Boxes* as the starting point for a matching and sorting activity. Take photos of a selection of toy cats and laminate them. Provide boxes, wicker baskets, small cushions and small pieces of cuddly fabric with the toy cats and give the children lots of time to explore and play. Observe the way in which the children use the resources and record the mathematical language used.

Dinosaur Roar!

Take the opportunity to introduce and model the use of descriptive vocabulary. Ask children for words that describe the size of dinosaurs, e.g. huge, enormous, gigantic, gargantuan or vast. Use decorators' brushes and buckets of paint to paint huge dinosaurs on lining paper and display these with the children's words in speech bubbles. Use a word cloud generator such as www.worditout.com or www.wordle.net to create a word cloud of the words children have suggested.

Extend the activity by inviting parents to contribute words with the children, and make a shared word cloud to be used by children, families and practitioners.

Wrapping presents

Support children's investigation of shape using a book about birthdays, such as *Kipper's Birthday*, as a starting point. Provide lots of toys to be wrapped, boxes, wrapping paper, sticky tape, labels, markers, ribbons and decorations. Encourage the children to estimate the amount of wrapping paper and ribbon needed to wrap the present.

Rosie's Walk

Provide magnetic sequence cards for the journey undertaken by Rosie. Encourage the children to retell the tale using positional language or ordinal numbers. Extend the activity as appropriate with children making individual zigzag books.

In the balance

Provide a balance and a variety of hard fruit and vegetables. Support children as they balance the food – one potato balances how many carrots? Can they find a way to record their findings?

Picnic time

Provide a picnic basket, several soft toys and a variety of picnic 'food'. Take turns to share the food fairly – what happens if there are four toys and six cakes? How many crisps will four toys get if there are 48 crisps altogether? How can three apples be divided?

Time's up

Provide a selection of objects in a shallow wicker basket, some tweezers and a sand timer. Ensure some of the items are easy to pick up with tweezers (e.g. soft wool balls, fabric squares) and include some that are more difficult (e.g. slippery or spherical objects). Set up a challenge: 'how many items can you move before the timer finishes?' and leave a clipboard with a list of the children's names.

Children must set off the sand timer and move objects out of the basket one at a time. Can they beat their own record? How will they record their score?

Use traditional tales as starting points for investigation outdoors.

Which beanstalk is the tallest?

Which beanstalk is the shortest?

The role of the adult

Most of children's understanding about number, shape and measures comes from talking about and exploring them through hands-on, fun, everyday experiences, and books and rhymes can be a great stimulus for this. Practitioners need to consider very carefully the following factors: the environment they provide, including ways in which to enrich continuous provision to value story and rhymes; specific, planned activities to support children's understanding through story and rhymes; the vocabulary they introduce and model through books; and the enabling statements and open-ended questions they ask.

Practitioners have a multifaceted role when supporting children's mathematical learning through stories and rhymes. They should:

- **Ensure number rhymes are used on a daily basis and introduced in a systematic manner – developing appropriate props e.g. magnetic props.**

- **Observe children's use of and interest in number rhymes.**

- **Observe children's exploration of maths from stories and fascination with specific books.**

- **Identify the mathematical content in traditional and contemporary stories and plan engaging experiences to support children's learning interests and needs.**

- **Help families to support children's developing use of number rhymes.**

- **Create interactive displays which support children's interest in number rhymes and stories with mathematical content.**

Maths home challenges

Goldilocks and the Three Bears

We've been learning about Goldilocks and the Three Bears.

See if you can find three teddy bears of different sizes in your house – if you can't find three, then choose any three cuddly soft toys.

Now look for three bowls and three spoons of different sizes together.

Take some time to play with these and talk about the bears, bowls and spoons:

- Which is the smallest bear?

- Which is the biggest bowl?

Perhaps you could make a bed for one of the bears – a box such as a shoe box is ideal.

Make your own book

Use the included folded A4 sheet to make your own zigzag counting book. Cut out some pictures of toys from catalogues. Stick one picture on the first page, two on the second, three on the third, and so on. Talk about the pictures together. Choose two toys – can you say something that is the same about them? What about something that is different?

Have fun!

Counting frogs

We've been learning a rhyme about five little frogs.

Copy and cut out frogs like the one on this sheet. Draw a log with your child and retell the rhyme together, moving the frogs as they 'jump into the water'.

Five little speckled frogs

Sat on a speckled log

Eating the most delicious grubs

Yum yum!

One jumped into the pool

Where it was nice and cool

Then there were four green speckled frogs

Glub, glub.

Chant the rhyme with your child – it's even more fun if you can find something to jump off into the 'water' – a tree stump or paving stone. If there are two of you, try using toys to make up five frogs!

Have fun!

Some counting books

10 Button Book by William Accorsi (Workman, 1999),

Anno's Counting Book by Mitsumasa Anno (Harper Collins, 1986),

Cleo's Counting Book by Stella Blackstone (Barefoot Books, 2007)

Handa's Hen by Eileen Browne (Walker, 2003)

1,2,3, to the Zoo by Eric Carle (Puffin, 1999)

The Monster Counting Book by Kate Daubney (Caterpillar, 2011)

Ten Little Monsters by Jonathan Emmett (Waterstones, 2005)

Ten Little Fingers and Ten Little Toes by Mem Fox (Walker, 2011)

Ten Little Ladybirds by Melanie Gerth (Gullane, 2008)

Counting, A child's first 123 by Alison Jay (Templar, 2008)

Ten Tiny Babies by Karen Katz (Little Simon, 2011)

We all went on Safari by Laurie Krebs (Frances Lincoln, 2003)

One Gorilla, a Counting Book by Atsuko Morozumi (Farrar, Straus & Giroux, 1993)

The Icky Bug Counting Board Book by Jerry Pallotta (Charlesbridge, 2008)

One is a Snail, Ten is a Crab by April Pulley Sayre and Jeff Sayre (Walker, 2004)

In my Garden by Ward Schumaker (Chronicle, 2005)

How Many Monsters? by Mara Van der Meer (Frances Lincoln, 2001)

March of the Dinosaurs by Jakki Wood (Frances Lincoln, 2007)

Words for possible core rhymes

When you begin to look at number rhymes, it becomes clear that there are many more rhymes for 'counting backwards' than there are for 'counting forwards'. You may want to devise your own with the children.

One elephant

One elephant went out to play

Upon a spider's web one day.

She had such enormous fun

That she called for another elephant to come.

Two elephants, three elephants . . .

Four elephants went out to play

Upon a spider's web one day.

They had such enormous fun

But there were no more elephants to come.

Five little men

Five little men in a flying saucer

Flew round the world one day

They looked left and right

And didn't like the sight,

so one man flew away.

Four little men, three little men, two little men, one little man.

One hungry dinosaur

One hungry dinosaur grazing in the sun

Roared out loud for a friend to come

Two hungry dinosaurs, three hungry dinosaurs, four hungry dinosaurs . . .

Five hungry dinosaurs grazing in the sun

Not expecting a Tyrannosaur to come

'Grr, Grr, Grr'

Five hungry dinosaurs all run away

No hungry dinosaurs are grazing today.

Five little speckled frogs

Five little speckled frogs

Sat on a speckled log

Eating the most delicious grubs

Yum! Yum!

One jumped into the pool

Where it was nice and cool

Then there were four green speckled frogs

Glug! Glug!

Four little speckled frogs, three little speckled frogs, two little speckled frogs, one little speckled frog.

Five little monkeys jumping on the bed

Five little monkeys jumping on the bed

One fell off and bumped his head

Phoned for the doctor and the doctor said

'No more monkeys jumping on the bed!'

Four little monkeys, three little monkeys, two little monkeys, one little monkey.

Five little monkeys and the crocodile

Five little monkeys

Sitting in a tree

Teasing Mr. Crocodile,

'You can't catch me'.

Along came Mr. Crocodile,

Quiet as can be

SNAP!

Four little monkeys, three little monkeys, two little monkeys, one little monkey.

Five little ducks

Five little ducks went swimming one day

Over the pond and far away

Mother duck said

'Quack! Quack! Quack! Quack!'

And only four little ducks came back

Four little ducks, three little ducks, two little ducks, one little duck . . .

Mother duck said

'Quack! Quack! Quack! Quack!'

And all the little ducks came swimming back.

One, two, three, four, five

One, two, three, four, five

Once I caught a fish alive

Six, seven, eight, nine, ten

Then I let it go again

Why did you let it go?

Because it bit my finger so!

Which finger did it bite?

This little finger on my right.

Peter hammers with one hammer

Peter hammers with one hammer, one hammer, one hammer,

Peter hammers with one hammer, all day long.

Peter hammers with two hammers, three hammers, four hammers, five hammers.

Make 'hammers' with body parts – starting with one hand, then two hands, add one and two feet, and finally the head as well.

Peter's going to sleep now, sleep now, sleep now,

Peter's going to sleep now, all night long.

Peter's waking up now, up now, up now,

Peter's waking up now, the whole day long.

Maths outdoors

Outdoor play gives children space to actively explore on a much larger scale.

Learning maths outdoors is an entitlement for all young children. Children play with and explore all kinds of maths ideas and skills when they are outside. In the outdoor area children are involved in working in the natural or built environment and they should be able to make more noise, indulge in more mess, engage with more speed and handle bigger objects. However, they will still need to be aware of a sense of order and they will need access to quiet areas for times when they want a rest from being climbers, runners, jumpers, riders and all-round superheroes.

Many children have limited access to outdoor play at home, and that many parents have anxieties about the safety of children playing outdoors. In some ways, our culture is taking outdoor play away from young children through the overwhelming prominence of technology and the perception of neighbourhoods as unsafe.

When planning for mathematics outdoors, it is worth recalling our own childhoods once again. Outdoor play is one of the things which actually characterizes childhood – indeed, many of our favourite childhood memories are of playing outdoors. What was it that made outdoor play different from indoor play? Of course, we could have played with our jigsaw puzzles, matchbox cars, Lego or dolls outside, but is that what we actually did? The answer is generally no – we don't simply repeat indoor play outdoors.

Outdoor play often included den building, tree climbing, making rose-petal perfume, collecting bugs, and assorted games with opportunities to yell, sing, explore, experiment, marvel, discover, take risks and create without the limits imposed by being indoors. When considering ways of developing maths outdoors, it is valuable to reflect on children's indoor experiences and think of ways to extend them outdoors, complementing and enhancing indoor provision and celebrating the unique qualities of the outdoor environment.

Help children to learn maths through all their senses: touch, smell, sound, sight and taste. Encourage the children to use natural materials for counting, sorting and measuring and to draw maps to find treasure. Plant seeds – you'll find lettuce grows quickly and is good to eat, and Russian sunflowers grow huge with tasty seeds. Wonder together at how many peas in a pod and Brussels sprouts on a stem. Paint with mud on a path or wall and wash it away with a hose. Do a survey of the trees, shrubs, flowers and minibeasts that lurk in your outdoor area. Support the children in describing what they see, be it a spider's web or a tree trunk, photograph it, draw it, or try touching it or using crayons to make a rubbing of it. Of course, all the chapters in this book have identified exciting and engaging outdoor activities for children, but this chapter focuses entirely on learning maths outdoors.

Extending indoor learning experiences outdoors

Occasionally, planning becomes over-complicated e.g. when different learning intentions for indoors and outdoors are identified. This is not necessary, or desirable, and certainly doesn't help children to make links in their learning or revisit their learning through different experiences and activities.

When the learning intentions for the week have been identified for maths, practitioners should plan experiences indoors and outdoors to support these. Think about experiences which are particularly successful indoors, and consider ways to extend them outdoors.

Number outdoors

Children will be counting lots of things indoors so look for imaginative ways to count outdoors.

- **Resource an area with large smooth pebbles (you can buy sacks of these from most garden centres) and use them for counting, making number lines, enclosing areas and patterning. Write numbers on some of them and try and make a l–10 line.**

- **Provide a selection of large, empty cardboard boxes. How many boxes can the children pile on top of each other before they fall down?**

- **Encourage the children to crawl inside the boxes – how many children can fit inside each box?**

- **Collect natural objects outdoors – who can be the first to collect 20 leaves or 10 twigs?**

- **Number games, for example, counting the number of children left 'in' and jumps on a number track.**

Measuring and mixing potions as part of role play outdoors.

Pattern outdoors

Indoors, children will be talking about, continuing, recreating and creating patterns on a small scale. Resource an area with forks, spoons, CDs and other materials to thread, and support children as they create a repeating-pattern wind chime or make repeating patterns with natural resources such as twigs, conkers and acorns. Outdoors:

- **Provide lots of large resources, including natural materials, to make a repeating pattern – crates, large boxes, logs, carpet squares and builders' buckets.**

- **Create an obstacle course with children, focusing on a repeating pattern.**

- **Make repeating patterns using wellington boot footprints in paint on wallpaper.**

- **Make living patterns – children in a line e.g. hands up, hands down, hands up, hands down.**

- **Make moving patterns – three hops, two jumps, three hops, two jumps.**

Measures outdoors

Indoors, children will be exploring length using small world equipment in their play.

Take the opportunity during children's play to line up cars, dinosaurs, plastic bears and other small world characters. When the children become interested in the lines you are making, lay down two pieces of ribbon a short distance apart and suggest the children fill the space between the two ribbons with some of the objects.

Outdoors:

- **With the children, choose a start and end point, for example, the outside door and the sand pit, or the outdoor house and the climbing frame. Line up the wheeled toys – how many wheeled toys is it between the two points? How many crates?**

- **Use non-standard measures, e.g. how many strides? How many pigeon steps between familiar objects?**

- **Living measures – children lay down, head to toe: how many body lengths from one point to another? How can this be recorded?**

- **Use narrow strips of lining paper to make some non-standard tape measures together, e.g. the length of a bike or a child lying down.**

Extending indoor role play to include outdoor role play

When planning indoor role-play scenarios to support mathematics, remember to extend the home corner to reflect the role play, and develop an outdoor role-play area which complements both. Wherever possible, try to include the wheeled toys in your planning. For example, for an AA or RAC rescue service, include tool boxes which contain maps, torches, number plates and signs to hang on vehicles.

Enhance home corner with:	Indoors	Outdoors
Smoke detector	Fire control office	Emergency vehicles
Vases/pots of flowers	Florist	Interflora delivery
First aid kit	Hospital	Paramedics
Pizzas and sauce bottles	Pizza restaurant	Take-away delivery
Tickets and brochures	Travel agency	Airport
Window box	Garden design	Garden centre
New toy pet	Vets	Pet rescue

Plan to include general resources, but also those which specifically support children's mathematical development. An outdoor building site and builders' merchant role play could include these materials to support mathematics:

- **shovels and buckets of different sizes, including builders' buckets**

- **tarpaulin and damp sand, gravel and pebbles**

- **large cardboard boxes, A-frames, ladders and planks**

- **hollow building blocks and play bricks**

- **guttering and pipes**

- **blankets, duvet covers to make 'roofs'**

- **numbered hard hats and wellington boots**

- **clipboards and markers to record plans**

- **standard and non-standard measuring sticks and tapes, balances and scales**

- **'money off' signs, vouchers and coupons**

- **telephone and directories**

- **loyalty cards, plastic and real coins, till, till receipts, invoices**

- **large cardboard box 'skips'**

Outdoor learning zones and resources which support mathematics

Mark-making

Ensure children have opportunities to make marks on a larger scale than indoors. Throw a curtain or sheet over a washing line and provide paints in squirty bottles. Encourage the children to squirt paint at the sheet and use large arm movement to create circles, lines and zigzag designs.

Promote mark-making by providing these 'must have' resources:

- **decorators' brushes and buckets of water**

- **playground chalk for marking on the ground**

- **large external chalk boards, fixed to the wall**

- **lining paper fixed to fences, paint and large brushes**

- **a wall area labelled 'Our mark-making area' for chalking**

- **A1 flip-chart paper on stands and easels**

- **clipboards and markers**

- **a range of different ground textures including paving slabs for graffiti writing**

Sound making and music

Give children opportunities to make noise on a larger and louder scale than indoors. Create the following:

- **Steel band – new, clean dustbins and dustbin lids, and beaters.**

- **Kitchen band – assorted saucepans, metal bowls and wooden spoons.**

- **Bucket band – assorted plastic buckets and bowls, with spoons and beaters.**

- **Hanging band – metal mugs, assorted pans, lengths of metal and plastic piping and metal plates attached to a washing line.**

- **Hand held recorders to record everyday outdoor sounds.**

Small equipment

Support children as they make up rules for games using small equipment, and explore tallying and scoring. Provide:

- quoits and hoops

- beanbags

- bats and balls

- assorted large balls

- plastic stilts and stepping stones

- cones

Large construction

Provide materials to build on a large scale and support children as they develop dens

- wooden blocks

- crates and tyres

- guttering, plastic pipes and cardboard tubes

- cardboard boxes

- rugs, blankets, duvet covers, lengths of fabric

- ties and pegs

- metal A-frames, planks and barrels

Playhouse and role play

Consider having a large, wooden outdoor playhouse built. Some role-play scenarios are particularly appropriate to outdoors, for example:

- stalls, e.g. fruit and vegetable

- outdoor or pavement café

- ice cream/hot dog/burger/kebab van

- garage/petrol station

- ship or train station

- farm or children's zoo

- bus and bus stops

- seaside

- construction site

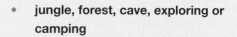

- jungle, forest, cave, exploring or camping

- outdoor concert stand

- AA or RAC rescue service

Climbing

- metal A-frames, planks and barrels

- fixed climbing equipment, including climbing walls

- natural things to climb

- ladders and slides

- wooden pallets

- tree trunk sections

Water play

- water channels

- guttering and plastic piping

- watering cans

- buckets, jugs , funnels and tubing

- water barrels, hosepipes

- opportunities to play in and sweep up puddles

Sand pit

- large shovels, buckets, jugs, garden sieves, watering cans

- large moulds and toys to support imaginative play

- natural objects – twigs, pebbles, shells and cones

Digging area and messy play

Extend indoor malleable and tactile play outdoors, where children can sometimes play more freely in a messy way. Provide:

- assorted shovels, spades, trowels and forks to dig

- garden sieves and assorted buckets

- wellington boots

- assorted bowls, saucepans, jugs with water, spoons

- gravel, pebbles, sand, potting compost to mix

- cornflour, bark chippings, wood shavings, to explore on a large scale

Growing area

- watering cans

- gardening tools, gloves

- flower and vegetable seeds, bulbs and plants

- fruit trees

- flower pots, planters and grow-bags

Games to play outdoors

Make use of the extra space outdoors to play lots of physical games. Taking part in a game can make maths meaningful for children and is a good way of learning maths in an interactive way. The outdoor area gives children opportunities to run around, make lots of noise, use balls, beanbags and quoits and experiment with ways of moving – hopping, jumping and skipping. Children who have lots of opportunities to join in with games introduced by adults can innovate, change the rules and make up games, creating new and better games of their own. Try to offer balls of different types and sizes , e.g. footballs, beach balls, sponge balls. Rolled up socks also make an easy 'ball' for younger children to catch. Involve yourself in playing with the balls and model how to use them. When you are kicking or throwing the balls talk about how far they went and discuss how high the ball was thrown. Compare the sizes and how heavy or light the balls feel.

As well as 'target games', think about parachute games, chalked games, track games and traditional games.

Using the whole body to find out more about shape and space.

Traditional games

- **Hopscotch**

- **Duck, duck, goose**

- **What's the time Mr Wolf?**

- **Isn't it funny how a bear likes honey?**

- **Sharks**

- **Sleeping lions**

- **Follow the leader**

- **Mr Crocodile**

Chalked games and track games

Chalked playground games are a great way to explore number, shape, space and measures. Other than a box of large playground chalk, very few resources are needed. Develop learning conversations during the game; discuss another way of playing the game or how it might start or finish. Help children to invent games that involve collecting and sorting different materials. Provide opportunities for children to explore counting through making large physical movements such as jumping, hopping and skipping along a track.

Chalked shapes

Draw a circle, square, rectangle and triangle on the ground. Make sure each shape is big enough for several children to stand in. Give the children lots of time to move around in different ways – hopping, jumping, crawling or walking backwards. Play some music, and call out one way of moving. When the music stops, call out the name of one shape and all children have to make their way to the correct shape. Extend the game by adding shapes of different colours, so that children have to move to the 'red circle' or 'blue square'. Make the game easier by holding up laminated cards with pictures of the shapes as you call out the shape's name. When the children are confident, let them take the lead.

Chalked numerals

Draw six chalked circles, with numerals 1–6 written inside them. Play the game as before, but when the music stops, call out a number name and children move to that circle. Extend the game by holding up cards with dice patterns on them. With smaller groups, throw a huge dice and call out the number together.

Unnumbered track games

Chalk a large unnumbered track with twenty squares. Place a potato on most of the squares, and more than one potato on some squares. Two to four children take turns to throw a huge dice and jump the number of squares along the track. If there is a potato on the square, they pick it up (only one). When the children have finished jumping along the track, count how many potatoes each has collected. Who has more, and who has fewer?

Extend the game by adding different objects, e.g. plastic cups to be collected on trays, beanbags in string bags, hats, shoes or handbags.

Musical cushions

Adapt the traditional game of musical chairs to play outdoors. Place the cushions in a line, making sure there are fewer cushions than children. Children move around the cushions clockwise and when the music stops, they must sit on a cushion. Any child without a cushion is out. Remove one or more cushions and continue. When there are only a few children and cushions left, make the route around them longer, perhaps by adding a cone at either end of the line. Support children as they make predictions about the number of children who will not have a cushion – what if there are six children and four cushions?

Parachute games – fruit salad

This is a large group or whole-class activity and children need time to become confident using the parachute. Allow time for just moving the parachute up and down, then add something like autumn leaves on the parachute, before playing more complex games.

All the children hold the parachute edge. Give each child the name of a fruit – try to think of 8–10 different fruits. As the children move the parachute up and down, call out one fruit. All the children allocated that fruit run under the parachute to change places. Try calling two fruit names at once, but make sure there are enough children holding the parachute. Let a child take the lead at calling fruit names. Put the parachute on the ground and call 'fruit salad' – all children run clockwise around the edge of the parachute and back to their place.

Extend the game and give the children names of animals, number names and shapes. Call out the name of the number or shape, or give the children clues such as 'a shape with three sides'; 'the number one more than three'.

Tallying and scoring

The outdoor area is a great place to support children as they develop their mark-making and use of mathematical graphics. Try to give children lots of opportunities to create their own systems and strategies for recording and solving maths situations, for example, keeping scores and tallying.

As you observe children using their own marks and tallies, encourage them to organize the marks to make counting easier. As children begin to use some representation of standard symbols, model the standard written form in a shared activity.

Provide support for tallying and keeping score:

- **pegs in a large biscuit tin – children fix one to the side of the tin**

- **pebbles in baskets – children move one pebble from a central store into their own small basket**

- **large markers and A1 flip pad**

- **airflow balls on strings fixed to the fence – move across to total score**

- **scoring with chalked tallies on the ground**

- **magnetic numerals on a magnetic wedge**

- **laminated numerals, spiral bound, which can be flicked over as the scores increase**

- **clipboards and markers**

Beanbags

Young children find beanbags much easier to throw and catch than balls so use these sometimes to throw through hoops or into buckets. Chalk targets on the ground – talk about how many points for each ring. Take turns to throw beanbags at the target. If you score one with the first beanbag and two with the second, how many points is this altogether?

Skittles

Fill ten empty bottles with water or sand. Set them out in a traditional triangular skittle formation – four in the back row, three in the next, two in the next and one at the front. If you knock down three skittles with the first ball, how many are left standing? Extend the activity to include calculations to 15 by adding another row of 5 skittles.

Balls in buckets

Set up six builders' buckets in a triangle. Choose a score for each bucket. Make up the rules together. Take turns to throw three balls into the buckets.

Dustbin lids

Take turns to throw rolled-up socks at a clean metal dustbin lid – listen to the noise it makes when the target is hit.

Teabags in paint

Fix some lining paper to the wall or a fence. Draw some huge targets. Take turns to throw used teabags, soaked in paint, at the targets. Each player uses a different colour. Who hits the bullseye the most times?

Tin-can alley

Collect empty tin cans and ensure they are clean and safe (with no sharp edges). Pile the cans, with three at the bottom, then two, then one. Take turns to knock the cans down, using rolled-up socks. How many can you knock down with one sock? How many can you knock down altogether?

Toy hoopla

Collect a selection of small soft toys and spread them out on the ground. Use wooden hoopla rings, or cut out hoops from corrugated cardboard. Take turns to throw the hoops over the toys – how many prizes can be won?

The role of the adult

As always, one of the key aspects of the adult role is to develop a stimulating environment with enriched areas of provision. In the outdoor area this means complementing and extending indoor provision, and celebrating the unique qualities of the outdoor environment, such as playing hide-and-seek games where children search for missing teddies, dinosaurs and numerals. It is important to remember that the adult role outdoors includes engaging as a co-player with children and extending learning; it is certainly not a 'hands-off' supervisory role. Practitioners need to plan to introduce, model and reinforce the use of specific vocabulary, and include enabling statements and open-ended questions about all aspects of mathematics learning (see individual chapters for specific ideas).

Organization

It is vital that outdoor play is available during all weathers, and that practitioners embrace the opportunities our diverse and unpredictable weather offers. Effective organization is absolutely fundamental. Consider:

- **resources stored in waterproof containers clearly labelled with words and pictures. Think about using coloured plastic dustbins to store large resources, so that they can be gathered together quickly when it rains**

- **wheeled trolleys to move equipment indoors**

- **wellington boots, waterproof coveralls and sun hats within easy reach**

- **outdoor learning zones clearly identified and planned for**

- **weather boxes to be stored and brought out to use as appropriate – windy, snowy, sunny and wet weather days**

- **areas to sit and chat – including moveable resources and materials to make 'dens'**

- **posters, charts, number lines, height charts and photos to support maths learning**

Recording in mathematics

Practitioners have an important role in supporting children's mathematical graphics and recording, both indoors and outdoors.

- **Take all opportunities throughout the day to model ways of recording mathematics, including the use of formal symbols – numerals. Outdoors, this will include writing scores.**

- **When acting as a co-player, model tallying – drawing four lines and a fifth line through to show a group of five, or with younger children, using symbols to record scores – three circles to represent three beanbags in a bucket perhaps.**

- **Provide a 'have a go' environment, where all children's mathematical graphics are valued and children have opportunities to experiment and practise recording in a variety of ways. Give children lots of time to explore so that they can become increasingly familiar and confident with recording.**

- **Use encouragements to record, e.g. 'how can we remember that?'**

- **Encourage children to talk about what they are doing and why – they need lots of time to talk about their recordings and think through how effective they are.**

Engaging with parents

It is very important that practitioners share the importance of learning outdoors with parents and families. In addition to anxieties about it being unsafe, some parents will be concerned that when children are outdoors, they are not 'learning'. We need to share our vision and values for outdoor learning, explaining what children are learning and how.

✦ **Create a display of images of children learning maths outdoors, with speech bubbles and comments from children and adults, and explanations of the learning taking place.**

✦ **Display digital photo frames or large scale screens with rolling picture-shows of outdoor learning.**

✦ **Show DVD footage of children learning maths outdoors – using natural resources, working on a much larger scale, learning collaboratively and taking the opportunities created by the weather.**

✦ **Create an oral history from both parents and children about their own outdoor play – remind them about the things they learned as they constructed dens or dams, invented new games and rules and explored and investigated.**

Aide memoire

Auditing whether the learning environment supports mathematical development

The indoor learning environment

- Are resources and working areas clearly labelled – with words, pictures or real objects where appropriate?

- Do displays include typed and handwritten numerals, by both adults and children?

- Do displays celebrate children's achievements in numbers, shape, space and measures and support children's future learning?

- Are there interactive displays/investigation areas which promote children's exploration of all areas of mathematics?

- Are resources that support mathematics high profile across areas of provision?

- Are children encouraged to use resources from the mathematic learning zone to support their learning in other areas of provision?

- Are there opportunities for children to match 3D objects to 2D silhouettes in storage? For example, water play, sand play.

- Are there books/cards with the words of number songs and rhymes in the music and sound-making area? With number props? For example, five frogs/ten in a bed.

- Are there empty boxes and packaging, reclaimed materials, and materials to encourage exploration of pattern in the creative workshop?

- Are books which support mathematics high profile in the book area? With story props?

- Are numerals explicit in small world, imaginative play? For example, road signs.

- Are there practical, hands-on opportunities to explore shape, space and measures? For example, sand, water, play dough, clay?

- Does the large block area/small construction area have visual images of things children can construct, photos of children's constructions and a range of construction equipment, including reclaimed materials?

The outdoor learning environment

- Does the outdoor environment complement and extend the indoor environment?

- Is the area well organized, inviting and challenging?

- Are there opportunities for children to be physical?

- Are there opportunities for children to be messy on a large scale?

- Are there opportunities for children to explore mathematics through movement? For example, obstacle courses, den making, travelling games, tracks, construction on a large scale?

- Can children access resources and return them independently?

- Is there a washing line at child height so that children can peg numerals in the correct order or socks/t-shirts to make repeating patterns?

- Are there opportunities to explore drawing shapes, patterns or numerals on a large scale? For example, chalking on floors, large scale chalk boards, easels, 'painting' with water and decorators' brushes.

- Are there permanent playground markings or chalked markings which support mathematics? For example, shapes, numerals, tracks.

- Is there a number line and height chart?

- Are there small resources and 'targets' to support scoring? For example, basket ball hoop, beanbags, quoits, skittles, knock-down cans.

- Are there resources to support the use of tallies or scoring?

Mathematics learning zone and reference area

- Are there story and information texts which support numbers for labels and for counting, calculating and shapes, space and measures?

- Is there a height chart showing standard and/or non-standard measures?

- Is there a number line which reflects children's interests displayed at child height – with picture clues where appropriate?

- Are resources clearly labelled so that children can access them independently?

- Is there a wide range of natural resources? For example, pebbles, fir cones, shells.

- Do children have access to a wide range of collections of everyday objects to explore? For example, ties, socks, balls, keys, coins, buttons, clocks and watches.

- Is there a wide range of commercially-produced resources to support exploration of numbers, calculating and shape, space and measures?

- Can children access games independently? For example, lotto, snap, dominoes, track games.

- Is there a display which draws attention to numerals in the environment/everyday life?

- Can children display their early attempts at recording independently?

- Is there a washing line at child height so that children can peg numerals in the correct order?

References and further reading

Aubrey, C. (1997), *Mathematics Teaching in the Early Years: An Investigation of Teachers' Subject Knowledge*. London: Routledge.

Biemiller, A. (2003), *'Vocabulary: needed if more children are to read well'*. Reading Psychology, 24, 323–3.

Bilton, H. (2005), *Playing Outside: Activities, Ideas and Inspiration for the Early Years*. London: Routledge.

Carruthers, E. and Worthington, M. (2006), *Children's Mathematics: Making Marks, Making Meaning*. London: Sage.

Cooke, H. (2007), *Mathematics for Primary and Early Years: Developing Subject Knowledge, (2nd ed.)*. London: Sage.

DCSF (2009), *Children Thinking Mathematically – PRSN essential knowledge for Early Years practitioners*. Nottingham: DCSF Publications.

DCSF (2008), *Mark Making Matters: Young children making meaning in all areas of learning and development*. Nottingham: DCSF Publications.

Gelman, R. and Gallistel, C. (1978), *The Child's Understanding of Number*. Cambridge, MA: Harvard University Press.

Gifford, S. (2005), *Teaching Mathematics 3–5; developing learning in the foundation stage*. Maidenhead: Open University Press.

Gunderson, E. A. and Levine, S. C. (2011), *'Some types of parent number talk count more than others: relations between parents' input and children's cardinal-number knowledge.'* Developmental Science, 14, 1021–32.

Hart, B. and Risley, T. R. (1995), *Meaningful Differences in the Everyday Experience of Young American Children*. Baltimore: Paul H. Brookes Publishing.

Haylock, D. and Cockburn, A. (2009), *Understanding Mathematics for Young Children*. London: Sage.

Hiebert, J., Linquist, M. M., Carpenter, T. P., and Fennema, E. (1997), *Making Sense: teaching and learning mathematics with understanding*. Portsmouth NH: Heinemann.

Holton, D. (1999), *Teaching Problem Solving*. Chichester: Kingsham Press.

Liebeck, P. (1990), *How Children Learn Mathematics: A Guide for Parents and Teachers*. London: Penguin.

Mason, J., Burton, L. and Stacey, K. (2010), *Thinking Mathematically (2nd ed.)*. London: Prentice Hall.

Montague-Smith, A. (2002), *Mathematics in Nursery Education*. Oxford: David Fulton.

Pound, L. (2006), *Supporting Mathematical Development in the Early Years*. Oxford: Oxford University Press.

Skemp, R. R. (1987), *Psychology of Learning Mathematics*. New York: Routledge.

Skinner, C. (2005), *Maths Outdoors*. Cheltenham: Nelson Thornes.

Stevens, J. (2008), *Maths in Stories*. Cheltenham: Nelson Thornes.

Stevens, J. (2010), Maths Now! The definitive guide to maths in the EYFS. Cheltenham: Nelson Thornes.

Thompson, I (ed.). (2008), *Teaching and learning early number (2nd ed.)* Maidenhead: Open University Press.

Williams, H. (2006), *Let's Pretend Maths*. Cheltenham: Nelson Thornes.

Williams, P. (2008). *Independent Review of Mathematics Teaching in Early Years Settings and Primary Schools* Nottingham: DCSF Publications.

Children's books referred to in activities

(see also book lists in Chapter 7)

Where's my Teddy? by Jez Alborough (Walker Books, 2004).

The Very Hungry Caterpillar by Eric Carle (Puffin, 2002).

The Doorbell Rang by Pat Hutchins (Harper Trophy, 1989).

Rosie's Walk by Pat Hutchins (Red Fox Picture Books, 2009).

The Giant Jam Sandwich by Vernon Lord and Janet Burroway (Boardbooks, 2009).

My Cat likes to Hide in Boxes by Eve Sutton (Puffin, 1978).

Websites

www.beam.co.uk/mathsofthemonth.php – challenging problems, open-ended investigations, and resources

www.early-education.org.uk – national voluntary organization for early years' professionals

www.earlylearningconsultancy.co.uk – downloadable resources including DfE publications

www.foundationyears.org.uk – a resource for those working in early years

www.ltl.org.uk – more about developing a stimulating outdoor environment

www.ncetm.org.uk – National Centre for Excellence in the Teaching of Mathematics

www.sign2learn.co.uk – Sign 4 Maths, using signing to support the understanding of the mathematical concepts and to remember vocabulary

www.worditout.com – create word clouds

www.wordle.net – create word clouds